Live the ADVENTURE

STEVE WINGFIELD

OLIVER
NELSON™

THOMAS NELSON PUBLISHERS
Nashville

Published in Nashville, Tennessee, by Thomas Nelson, Inc.

Unless otherwise noted the Bible version used in this publication is the HOLY BIBLE: NEW INTERNATIONAL VERSION®. Copyright © 1973, 1978, 1984 by International Bible Society. Used by permission of Zondervan Publishing House. All rights reserved. The author has capitalized diety pronouns for emphasis.

Scripture quotations noted NKJV are from THE NEW KING JAMES VERSION. Copyright © 1979, 1980, 1982, Thomas Nelson, Inc., Publishers.

ISBN 0-7852-6774-3

Printed in the United States of America

1 2 3 4 5 6 QWD 06 05 04 03 02 01

I dedicate this book to Barb, my wife of 26 years, and Michelle and David, our two children. Their belief in me, their encouragement, support, and understanding have helped me become the man I am in Christ. It is a joy, an honor, and a privilege, beyond my ability to describe, to *Live The Adventure* with my family. I love you and because of Christ and the three of you, I am blessed!

CONTENTS

INTRODUCTION

If you enjoy listening to Steve Wingfield preach, you will enjoy reading his book. Why? Because reading his book is just like listening to his sermons. As I read this manuscript, I felt the heart of Steve Wingfield because he writes like he preaches.

Steve's sermons are easy to understand, so this is an easy book to read. You will find yourself easily going from one paragraph to another, just as you listen to Steve go from one point to another in his sermons.

His ideas are down to earth, "where you live" if you are a common working American. You will find illustrations from the normal life, as well as practical applications that help you live for Jesus Christ. The best part of all is that the book is Bible-based. If you have ever heard Steve Wingfield preach, you know he refers to the Word of God again and again.

Just as Steve's preaching presents Jesus Christ to unsaved people, you will see Jesus Christ in the first two or three chapters of this book. I love the fact that he begins Chapter One with *He is Looking for You,* meaning God was searching for you long before you searched for Him. So notice how the book unfolds. In the next chapter you will find out that God's favorite word is "come." The following chapter tells about God's love and the forgiveness from sin that He gives you.

I have attended several "Encounters" where Steve Wingfield has presented the gospel of Jesus Christ. Whereas some preachers are great in oratory, and other preachers are deep theologians, you get the impression that he is talking to you on a one-to-one basis. His sermons are personal, and so is this book.

Steve Wingfield has targeted small towns in America with his evangelistic encounters. Why? He told me, "I want the Encounter to be the biggest event that happens in that town that year." While it may take a Billy Graham to be the biggest religious event in a large metropolitan area, Steve Wingfield is able to rally the churches so that *Encountering Jesus* is the biggest event that year for that town.

I teach a Sunday School class of about one thousand people. In June 2000 Steve Wingfield taught my Sunday School class in the auditorium of Thomas Road Baptist Church in Lynchburg, Virginia. That is the auditorium where Steve Wingfield came to know the Lord Jesus Christ. As he taught the class, he pointed back to the left-hand side where he sat that night as an unsaved young man. He did not attend willingly. A member of the church had "badgered" young Wingfield into attending the crusade. That night the Holy Spirit convicted Steve Wingfield and he walked forward to receive Jesus Christ as his Savior and his life was forever changed.

Almost immediately Roy Dillard, still a member of my class, began taking Steve Wingfield to different evangelistic crusades in small churches in central Virginia. Each time Steve gave his testimony, many people were converted. It was evident to all that God had anointed Steve as an evangelist from the moment he was converted. Within weeks of receiving Jesus Christ, Steve Wingfield began preaching in churches and on some occasions there were twenty people that responded to the gospel invitation.

Many of Steve Wingfield's friends visited my class that day when I had Steve Wingfield teach for me. Many who had been converted under his ministry wanted to come back "home" to hear him present the gospel once again. During the next two or three weeks, many people in other churches who were not able to attend that day contacted me to tell how they too had been converted under Steve Wingfield's ministry. Now I know that God has called him to be an evangelist.

Whenever Steve Wingfield leaves a town, many will remember him and the encounter where they met Jesus Christ. May you enjoy reading *Live the Adventure* as much as I did. Then may you go live the adventure with Jesus Christ.

ELMER L. TOWNS
Lynchburg, Virginia

HE IS LOOKING FOR YOU

The nation was riveted to the network news special report. A cultural icon was lost at sea. Hours turned to days as military ships, airplanes, and helicopters crisscrossed a small portion of the Atlantic Ocean. They combed the waters, looking for signs of John F. Kennedy Jr.'s tragic plane crash. The president issued an order to find the lost pilot and his family members at any cost. An important person was lost and had to be found.

Early on the fifth day of the search, divers aided by navy sonar equipment finally located the wreckage.[1] Hours later, the remains of the crash victims were tenderly brought to the surface. The nation's fears were confirmed: JFK Jr. was dead. The search ended in deep sorrow.

Not long ago, near my home in the beautiful Shenandoah Valley of Virginia, a young boy wandered away from home and was lost in the mountains. News of the emergency spread quickly through the community. More than one hundred volunteers and rescue workers searched long into the night. Concern for the little boy's life grew as temperatures dropped below freezing in the mountains of Virginia. Could he survive such a night? Many people risked their safety as they searched through the rugged mountains trying to find the lost boy. But I am thankful to report that this story had a happy ending.

In my mind, I can still clearly see the news clips as the police officer walked out of the woods holding the little boy in his arms. Locked in my memory is the sight of the boy's mother and father arriving at the scene in a police car. They jumped from the car as it was rolling to a stop. Running to their son with tears of joy flowing down their cheeks, they thanked God and everyone who had helped with the search. They were overcome with joy. The boy was unharmed. He had been protected from the cold night by the warmth of his big dog's body as they cuddled together.

Words are not adequate to describe such a moment. That family's joy and peace of mind must be experienced to fully appreciate the thrill of finding and being found. The search was over, and it had been successful. The little boy was safe and unharmed. A relationship was restored. It was a joy-filled moment.

YOUR GREATEST SEARCH

Whether it's a search for a famous person or a local boy lost in the woods, the intensity of a search captivates our attention and emotions. Many men and women are on an even more desperate search—a search for God. Their search has become a national emergency in their lives as they use every possible resource, trying to find the answer to their deepest needs. They look for Him in the wilderness of loneliness and suffering. They cry out to Him from painful, broken relationships. They wonder where He is or whether He exists in the midst of their shattered dreams. They look for Him during traumatic career changes or sudden financial crises. They ask, "Where is God?" Life seems to be falling apart before their eyes.

Others look for God in "spiritual places." They search for His presence in stately cathedrals or in places of solitude. Some walk the surf, searching for Him and hoping that the pounding waves will somehow connect them with the God of the universe. Others have tried to commune with Him on a rugged mountain, straining to hear His voice.

Desperately, through what seem to be endless hours of loneliness and pain, people search for something or someone to fill the aching voids of their hearts. In our world, many have searched for happiness, fulfillment, and peace of mind in all the wrong places.

Sound familiar? Where have you been looking? You might have thought you had a firm handle on life when suddenly you lost your grasp. The life that seemed to make sense is now a hazy, senseless existence. You feel as if you are driving through a blizzard and life is now incomprehensible. You want fulfillment and happiness. Deep down, we all do. "But where do I look for an answer to all my problems?" you ask. "Would God accept me? Could He make a difference in my life? Could it be true that God loves me?"

There are hundreds of dead-end streets on the road to fulfillment and peace. If you listen to the gods of this world, you will be tempted to follow all the wrong paths. No matter how many dead ends you've reached in your life, you must step back and take an honest look at what they promise. If you believe every claim the world offers along your way, you will be tempted to believe that you can find peace and fulfillment in all kinds of things. More money, a new car, a drink, or a new pill may promise to fill that void. The latest craze always draws people who search for help. If you believe the TV ads, a psychic will provide the answer to your search. In many social circles, people brag about time spent with their analysts. Yet if most are honest with you and themselves, they admit that peace and contentment continue to evade their grasp. Perhaps you have tried all of these roads and more, and to tell the truth, you're still searching.

Maybe your search has included God. You have known about Him. Perhaps you can remember going to church as a child. You have always known that He loves you, but you have never included Him in your life. You know the need is there, yet you plan to deal with that later. You've cried out to Him in a moment of crisis. Maybe you've called out His name in anger and frustration. Still, your emptiness remains.

Maybe you can identify with a forty-year-old man I met recently. On a material scale, he was the successful manager of a flourishing retail store. He had a great salary, a nice car, fine clothing, and a beautiful home, but his life was empty of meaning and purpose. He was filled with fear, hurt, and bitterness. He knew virtually nothing about God. He had heard of God's love, but he was not ready to accept it. "After all," he reasoned, "I have been so bad, God would never want anything to do with me."

Finally the pain became so intense he had nowhere else to turn. As a last resort in his search for meaning and purpose, he decided to give God a try and he walked into a church where I was speaking. After the service he said, "This was the first time in my life I have ever entered a church building."

I told him, "God has a plan for your life. He longs to live in relationship with you."

"Let me get this straight," he said. "You are telling me God loves me? Even after all I have done? He will forgive me and accept me? I can be free of this guilt? Why doesn't everybody want to know Him?"

Have you taken an honest look at God? Or have you chosen

to believe the gods of this world? They scream at us from every direction: "Try me!" or "This will be the thing that brings you happiness," or "If you want inner peace, get this," or "If you're looking for fulfillment, you must do this, have that, or go there."

Let's be honest—you know that none of this stuff has worked. None of it has taken away the loneliness and emptiness. God designed you to live in relationship with Him. Until you experience His love in a personal way, there will always be a void in your life. You can try to fill that void with all kinds of aspirations and relationships, but none of it will work. Regardless of how successful or full your life becomes, you will always hunger for more.

All of us have a God-shaped vacuum, and we go through life trying to fill that vacuum. Until we find God and allow Him to fill the vacancy in our lives, we will always have an inner emptiness. The void is reserved for His presence. God created you to live in fellowship with Him. Not until you come into a relationship with the living God can you reach your fullest potential.

You can experience success—as defined by this world—without God. But you will find no fulfillment in the world's greatest versions of success. Several years ago I was in the office of a successful businessman who is regarded as a national business leader. Buildings have been named after him; he has received many awards from business and civic organizations; he owns houses and vacation resorts around the country. He told me, "I climbed the ladder of success. I got to the top and found out there is nothing here. But as I climbed the ladder, I left behind my wife and my children. Now they want nothing to do with me."

You can gain fame without God. There is another picture locked in my mind each time I think of the fleeting and fickle nature of fame. Years ago, a man was running for president of the

United States of America. He won his party's nomination, and everywhere he went, the film was rolling and microphones captured his every word. Everyone wanted to hear what he had to say, but he was soundly defeated in the election. Four years later at his party's convention, the press corps followed someone else. *Newsweek* captured a picture of the former candidate. He was leaning against a back wall at the convention, completely alone. The look on his face said it all. Fame had passed him by, and no one seemed to care what he had to say. Yes, you can have fame without God, but not lasting fulfillment.

You can experience pleasure without God. The Bible is very honest in noting that there is pleasure in sin for a period of time. The Bible says that Moses "chose to be mistreated along with the people of God rather than to enjoy the pleasures of sin for a short time" (Heb. 11:25). Yes, you can experience pleasure without God. But I contend that you will never know true contentment and fulfillment without knowing God. Lasting pleasure comes only from knowing Him.

Why are you searching? Do you believe that by finding Him, you will have a stronger sense of purpose? What are you looking for? Inner healing? A break from past failure? Hope for the future? Love and acceptance?

Deep inside, you believe that finding Him means more than anything else in the world. This relationship is more valuable than wealth. All the success and wealth this world offers cannot compare to the value of a relationship with God.

Being famous means having a lot of people recognize you when they see you. Quite frankly, when the chips are down, I want God to know me. Finding God is far more fulfilling than achieving fame. Think about it. God knows me! Success, pleasure, and fame are irrelevant in comparison.

Your relationship with God is far more important than any other relationship. When you find Him, your life will have a sense of wholeness.

GOD IS SEARCHING TOO

There is good news! God has been looking for you a lot longer than you have been looking for Him. As you read the Bible, you will come to understand that it is all about God's search for you. Of course, God knows where you are at all times; He "will neither slumber nor sleep" (Ps. 121:4).

Two of God's attributes are omnipresence and omniscience. *Omnipresence* means He is everywhere at the same time. As human beings, we have a difficult time understanding that concept because we have no reference point with which to compare it. We are limited to time and space; we can be in only one place at one time.

Omniscience means God is all-knowing. He knows everything about us. Maybe you don't want to think about that, but God sees everything we do. There are no secrets. God knows every thought, every word, every action. He is God, and you and I cannot escape His knowledge.

Even though God knows all the rebellion and fickleness in you and me and all of humanity, He longs to live in relationship with us. He wants you to know Him personally. He desires to fill the God-shaped vacuum in your life. He created you to fellowship with Him, and He longs for you to find fulfillment, joy, and peace in knowing Him.

You may not recognize His presence in your life. You may not understand what He is like or how much He loves you. Nevertheless, He has gone to the greatest lengths to find you and to establish a loving and lasting relationship with you. God's "search and rescue" makes any similar effort on earth pale in comparison.

THE GREATEST SEPARATION

Why is God searching for you? How did you become separated from Him in the first place? Someone once wrote, "What is there about man that causes him to alienate himself from his own good intentions, from his neighbor and from his God? Whatever it is, it is something from within."

Why the separation? He created us. He provides for us. He loves us unconditionally. We speak to Him. We trust Him during crises. Why are we separated from Him?

There's a classic story about a child who disobeyed his parents. Finally his mother took him over to the "quiet time" area and asked him to sit in a chair. "You sit there until you learn to behave!" she commanded.

The little boy obeyed and was silent for a while. But he soon spoke up, "Mother, I just want you to know that I may be sitting down on the outside, but inside, I'm standing up!"

We are born with a tendency to "stand up on the inside." We want to act without regard for what God wants. We choose to live in disobedience rather than obedience to God. We choose to follow our wills rather than to seek God's will for our lives. That "stand up on the inside" attitude is called sin.

Sin is breaking God's law on purpose. First, we know what God's law is, as revealed in His Word, the Bible. Second, we make a decision to disobey the known law of God. Third, we act on that decision in behavior that is contrary to His perfect will for us. "Everyone who sins breaks the law; in fact, sin is lawlessness" (1 John 3:4). God created us to have a loving relationship with Him. But this disobedience causes a spiritual separation—spiritual distance, distrust, confusion, awkwardness, and fear.

We see that principle played out in the lives of the very first inhabitants of the world, God's created man and woman, Adam and Eve: "God said, 'Let us make man in our image, in our likeness, and let them rule over the fish of the sea and the birds of the air, over the livestock, over all the earth, and over all the creatures that move along the ground.' So God created man in His own image, in the image of God He created him; male and female He created them" (Gen. 1:26–27).

Not only did God create them perfectly, He put them in a perfect environment: "Now the LORD God had planted a garden in the east, in Eden; and there He put the man He had formed. And the LORD God made all kinds of trees grow out of the ground—trees that were pleasing to the eye and good for food" (Gen. 2:8–9).

God lovingly watched over His creation. He provided food for their bodies and fellowship for their spirits. And all that He asked in return was that they abstain from eating of one tree in the Garden—the Tree of Knowledge of Good and Evil. He said, "You must not eat from the tree of the knowledge of good and evil, for when you eat of it you will surely die" (Gen. 2:17).

Why would God make such a requirement? Why would He tempt Adam and Eve in that way? All of us would be naturally curious; we would want a taste of that fruit just because it was forbidden. But that wasn't natural to Adam and Eve. Their first thoughts were complete obedience.

Why bother eating from that tree?

God doesn't want us to, and He has given us plenty of other trees to pick from.

Before the first act of disobedience to God—the first sin—obedience and trust defined our relationship with God. When sin severed that close relationship, disobedience, doubt, fear, and skepticism described humanity's lack of relationship with God.

God gave Adam and Eve freedom and responsibility in their new world, and He gave them the right of ultimate choice—to choose to obey Him. Why did He give them this choice? Because He wanted them to love and trust Him *on their own initiative*. True love does not force or coerce love.

Just as people *sin* against God *on purpose*, so we can *love and trust* Him *on purpose*.

THE GREATEST DECEPTION

I'm sure you have heard the common expression, "The devil made me do it!" Adam and Eve could have said the same thing. The devil, also known as Lucifer or Satan, was a created being—actually an angel in heaven—who led a rebellion of angels against God and was thrown out of heaven (Isa. 14:12).

Satan now resides in an evil spirit world, where his intent is to destroy everyone and everything that God loves. Paul explained to the young believers, "You were dead in your transgressions and sins, in which you used to live when you followed the ways of this world and of the ruler of the kingdom of the air, the spirit [the devil] who is now at work in those who are disobedient" (Eph. 2:1–2).

A cloud of doubt marred Adam and Eve's ideal setting. Satan came into the garden in the form of a serpent: "Satan himself masquerades as an angel of light" (2 Cor. 11:14). Satan spoke to Eve, and she began to doubt what God had said:

Now the serpent was more crafty than any of the wild animals the LORD God had made. He said to the woman, "Did God really say, 'You must not eat from any tree in the garden'?" The woman said to the serpent, "We may eat fruit from the trees in the garden, but God did say, 'You must not eat fruit from the tree that is in the middle of the garden, and you must not touch it, or you will die.'" "You will not surely die," the serpent said to the woman. "For God knows that when you eat of it your eyes will be opened, and you will be like God, knowing good and evil." When the woman saw that the fruit of the tree was good for food and pleasing to the eye, and also desirable for gaining wisdom, she took some and ate it. She also gave some to her husband, who was with her, and he ate it. (Gen. 3:1–6)

The seeds of doubt were sown. Eve questioned God's motives: "Why would God keep anything from us? What is He holding back? Maybe if I eat from this tree, I can be more like God and understand everything!"

Sin begins with disobedience in our minds, and once we have disobeyed mentally, it's a small step to act on it. Sin is choosing to disobey God. When we choose to live in sin, we choose to live in spiritual separation from God. God said to Adam and Eve, "If you eat of the fruit, you will die."

Before sin entered this world, there was no death, only life. Because of their sin, Adam and Eve experienced two kinds of death. The immediate death was spiritual. The other—physical death—happened over time. Adam and Eve were no longer living in fellowship with God. Their sinful choice caused spiritual separation from their Creator.

The tree and its fruit looked beautiful and safe, and they

probably were. But Adam and Eve were outside God's plan. Even their desire to gain wisdom and to be more like God wasn't bad in itself. Sin was choosing to do it their way instead of trusting God's love and plan for their lives.

Notice the progress of disobedience. Eve disobeyed God, and she influenced Adam to disobey as well. Sin doesn't like to act on its own; it wants a partner, someone to back up the disobedient decision—promising safety in numbers, as it were.

THE GREATEST QUESTION

God's reaction to this first sin was not to bring harsh punishment on Adam and Eve—to *zap them!* What did He do? He went looking for them! "The man and his wife heard the sound of the LORD God as He was walking in the garden in the cool of the day, and they hid from the LORD God among the trees of the garden. But the LORD God called to the man, 'Where are you?'" (Gen 3:8–9).

Remember, God is omniscient. He knew where Adam and Eve were, but He wanted them to realize that He was looking for them. He also wanted them to respond to Him, to admit what they had done. The Bible has a word for admitting our disobedience to God. It's a word that also means to be sorry enough for disobeying that we decide not to do it again. It's *repent.* "Repent, then, and turn to God, so that your sins may be wiped out, that times of refreshing may come from the Lord" (Acts 3:19). Notice the result: your sins are "wiped out," and you receive "times of refreshing." God always seeks to give us His best.

Adam answered God's question in a strange way: "I heard you in the garden, and I was afraid" (Gen. 3:10). Adam and Eve had been in the habit of talking freely with God; now they were hiding in fear. They once enjoyed the company of God; now they were distressed by it. They once enjoyed a spirit of freedom; now they lived in bondage.

Their sin also affected their relationship with one another. God asked another important question: "Have you eaten from the tree that I commanded you not to eat from?" (Gen. 3:11). Having turned from God, they turned on each other: "The man said, 'The woman you put here with me—she gave me some fruit from the tree, and I ate it'" (Gen. 3:12).

When our relationship with God is broken, all of our relationships are adversely affected. Living in guilt and shame results in our distrust of others. The presence of sin can destroy the deepest human bond of love.

"Where are you?"

God searched for Adam and Eve, even while they were hiding from Him. God never stopped loving them, even though they sinned. God spoke of His love for His people: "I have loved you with an everlasting love; I have drawn you with loving-kindness" (Jer. 31:3). From the moment of that first sin, God has been working to restore the original relationship of love and trust with us.

God asks the same question of you: "Where are you?" Are you hiding, alone with guilt over some past disobedience? Are you hiding, alone with feelings of distrust?

The good news is, God is looking for you!

THE GREATEST CONSEQUENCE

The analogy has been made that a judge who could excuse a crime would not be considered a just judge. In law, an appropriate consequence is applied to every crime. That is justice. It is the same in the spiritual realm. Breaking God's law has an appropriate consequence.

Adam and Eve could have been excused from their disobedience. But that excuse would have been a betrayal of the trust God had established with them. To be a just God, a just partner in their relationship, God had to keep His word. There could be no exceptions. There had to be a consequence. If He excused one sin, no one would ever be convinced that God hates sin or that obedience is important to Him.

For Adam and Eve, the greatest consequence of sin was spiritual separation from God (spiritual death), and for the first time, ultimate physical death entered the world. They were also banished from the Garden of Eden, the Paradise that God had created for them: "So the LORD God banished him [Adam] from the Garden of Eden to work the ground from which he had been taken" (Gen. 3:23). An additional consequence for Adam was a life of toil, and Eve suffered the consequence of painful childbirth (Gen. 3:16). The consequences were passed on to future generations, including us. Toil and suffering are inevitable. Along with the judgment of toil and suffering came sin and separation from God.

THE GREATEST REMEDY

The first couple's disobedience was a terrible tragedy for them, and their choice affected all of humanity. But with the tragedy of sin came the awesome mercy of God.

Once Adam and Eve walked the Garden of Eden in unclothed innocence. After disobeying God's law, the Bible says they were "naked" and "afraid" (Gen 3:10). They had lost their innocence. What was God's reaction? Loving mercy! "The LORD God made garments of skin for Adam and his wife and clothed them" (Gen. 3:21). God allowed the first shedding of blood to cover Adam and Eve's guilt and fear.

God made a provision of forgiveness, even though Adam and Eve had turned their backs on Him. He never stopped looking for them, longing to reestablish the relationship that was lost in their sinful disobedience. He met them where they were and gave them what only He could give—the provision of His restoration.

And in His provision for Adam and Eve, God provided for all of us. At the very "crime scene," He provided the ultimate pardon. God's *greatest remedy* was in the form of a prophecy that was given to Satan, disguised as a serpent. He said,

> I will put enmity
>> between you and the woman,
>> and between your offspring and hers;
> he will crush your head,
>> and you will strike his heel. (Gen. 3:15)

God promised a go-between. Someone would be supernaturally born, the "offspring" of a woman, who would "crush" the intentions of Satan, even though Satan would "strike" (wound) Him.

Who would He be? The Lord Jesus Christ!

In God's search for our hearts, He eventually offered His only Son. Jesus was born as a man to live among us without disobeying God. As a perfect sacrifice, Jesus bore the complete punishment for all of our sins by His innocent death on the cross.

Through God's remedy, we can reestablish our relationship with God:

> For it pleased the Father that in Him all the fullness should dwell, and by Him to reconcile all these things to Himself, by

Him, whether things on earth or things in heaven, having made peace through the blood of His [Christ's] cross. (Col. 1:19–20 NKJV)

For God so loved the world that He gave His one and only Son, that whoever believes in Him shall not perish but have eternal life. For God did not send His Son into the world to condemn the world, but to save the world through Him. (John 3:16–17)

It is vital for you to know that God is looking for you. I am praying that you are looking for God. If you are, claim this promise from God Himself. It was originally written to King Solomon, but it is a truth that applies to all humanity: "Acknowledge the God of your father, and serve Him with wholehearted devotion and with a willing mind, for the LORD searches every heart and understands every motive behind the thoughts. If you seek Him, He will be found by you" (1 Chron. 28:9).

2

GOD'S FAVORITE WORD IS *COME*

I believe God has a favorite word: *Come!* It must be a special word since He uses it so often throughout the Bible. "Come to Me," Jesus told the little children whom the disciples tried to send away (Mark 10:14). "Come, all you who are thirsty, come to the waters," invited the prophet (Isa. 55:1). "Come to Me, all you who are weary and burdened," called Jesus to the crowds (Matt. 11:28).

Most of us have received a special invitation. I remember the first time my dad asked me to go trout fishing with him. As a boy in rural Virginia, I grew up loving the outdoors. I had often seen my dad bring home a string of fish. He cleaned them, Mom fried them for supper, and we had a feast. Dad had taken me fishing in my uncle's pond many times, but I had never gone trout fishing. It was a very special invitation because I would be allowed to miss a day of school.

I still remember my excitement the morning of our fishing day. We all got up early and packed our supplies and lunches. Mom made a great breakfast for us. We met some friends and drove to the Piney River in the beautiful mountains of Virginia. I was surprised at the number of people who were at the river. We found our spot and waited until noon, when trout season offi-cially opened. The excitement was electric. I could hardly contain myself. A Virginia game warden walked along the bank, making sure no hooks were in the water too soon.

Twelve o'clock finally arrived. I can still hear my dad say, "Let's catch a fish!" I am sure it was providential—I know it was not skill—but somehow, I caught the first fish that beautiful April afternoon. Locked in my memory are the vivid pictures of that wonderful spring day on the banks of Piney River in Amherst County, Virginia. Most of my friends were in school, but I was with my dad fishing. Life couldn't get any better for a six-year-old boy. What a gift: to receive the invitation to "come" from someone who has our best interest at heart!

Do you realize that God wants to spend time with you? He longs to live in relationship with you. He wants what is best for you, and He is totally committed to helping you become the person He created you to be. He is not some distant god that has no interest in you. He is a personal God who wants to be involved in your life.

Many people do not have memories of a good relationship with their dads. If you are one of them, my heart aches for you. I wish I had the power to erase all your bad memories. Of course, I can't, but I encourage you not to transfer those bad memories of your earthly dad to God. He is not a God to be feared in the sense that some fear their abusive or absent earthly fathers. Take a moment to imagine what the best image of a perfect earthly father would be for you. God, our heavenly Father, is far better than any ideal you could imagine.

He wants to live in a loving relationship with His creation, including you and me. King David had a close relationship with God. In fact, God called David "a man after my own heart" (Acts 13:22). God also inspired David to write poetry. In Psalm 139:13–14, he wrote,

For you created my inmost being;

    You knit me together in my mother's womb.

I praise You because I am fearfully and wonderfully made;

    Your works are wonderful,

    I know that full well.

Not only did God create us, He has made Himself known to us through His Son, the Lord Jesus Christ. He calls us to Himself. To every person in the world, He says, "Come."

God longs

- to be reconciled to us. Come and be forgiven (Col. 2:13).

- to deliver us from oppression. Come and be set free (John 8:32).

- to make us whole. Come and be purified (1 John 1:9).

- to free us from our burdens. Come and be healed (Matt. 8:17).

COME TO WHAT?

God invites us to come and experience life at its best. In His presence there is peace, even in the worst situations. God says to you, "Come and allow Me to help you become the person I created you to be." When you respond to God's invitation, He will begin producing the fruit of the Spirit in your life: "The fruit of the Spirit is love, joy, peace, patience, kindness, goodness, faithfulness, gentleness and self-control" (Gal. 5:22–23). Take an honest look at your life—just take a moment to pull the curtain back and examine your heart. Do you see evidence of the fruit of the Spirit in your life?

Do the peace and love of God's presence describe what's inside you? I can't see inside your heart, and neither can anyone else. Those close to you know what you are like most of the time, but even they cannot see inside your heart. Guess what? God sees it all! But even after seeing it all, He still loves you. He is totally committed to helping you become all that you can be in Him.

My dad and I planted a tree one spring that reminds me of the fruit of the Spirit. It was an apple tree—but not just any apple tree. This one apple tree produced five varieties of apples. It was a novelty and the apples were very tasty. Several years after we had planted the special tree, Dad and I decided to conduct an experiment. And believe it or not, it worked. We grafted two types of pear trees onto the apple tree. Both grafts lived, and we had a tree that produced five different kinds of apples and two types of pears. It was quite a sight. When people came to visit our home, I took them to see our special tree. I can still see the amazed looks on their faces. How is this possible? Well, I don't understand the scientific explanation, but I know it worked. I told people, "God did it."

You may read the list of great qualities from Galatians 5 and ask, "How is it possible for the fruit of the Spirit to be produced in my life? I just pulled the curtain back on my heart, and it was not a pretty sight." That is exactly why all of us need to accept God's invitation to come and live in relationship with Him. How is all this possible? Well, God's working in your life is a bit like what happened with the apple tree. I can't explain it all, but I know it works. I could give you a long and detailed theological explanation, but I doubt that is what you want. Basically, we respond to His call to come, and He then begins working in our lives to make us into the people He created us to be. As He works in us, our lives begin to show the evidence of His working. It is just as real as standing in my parent's backyard, seeing those five varieties of apples along with two kinds of pears on the same tree. People can see the fruit of the Spirit being produced in our lives.

He says, "Come live a full and meaningful life within My plan." As Jesus told the religious teachers, "I have come that they [believers] may have life, and have it to the full" (John 10:10). The word *full* here, literally translated from Greek, the language in which the New Testament was written, means more than the English word, full. We think of "full" as maximum volume or complete, but the Greek word is a lot more than the opposite of "empty." When Jesus offers us "full life" in this verse, He is describing a life of meaning, purpose, and direction. That is why Jesus wants us to respond to His invitation. He wants us to experience a life that is full with these qualities.

THE MOST IMPORTANT INVITATION

God issues the most important invitation anyone can ever receive. I thank God daily that I responded to His call. It was the best decision I have ever made. I am much younger than my six brothers and sisters. By the time I was eight years old, my dad was a minister, and my four brothers were already involved in full-time ministry or were preparing to enter the ministry. I felt that wherever I went, people asked, "Are you going to be a pastor too?" I responded to this pressure by rejecting the Lord and His plan for my life.

By the time I was twenty-one, I was in full-blown rebellion, and I rarely went to church. I had quit going to college and was working as a safety investigator at a large nuclear power plant. When I arrived at work one Wednesday morning, Bill, a friend who worked in the same office, invited me to attend church with him that evening. I made an excuse and refused. Later that morning, he started telling me about the evening's speaker and again invited me to go with him. "Bill, I am not going," I said. At lunch, Bill sat across from me, and once again, he started talking about how good the speaker was and how much he thought I would enjoy hearing him. I got mad and left the table.

That afternoon, Bill came to my desk and apologized. He said he didn't want to damage our friendship and was really sorry that I was upset. I told him not to worry—everything was okay. With tears in his eyes he said, "Steve, I'm just concerned, and I really would like you to go with me." I threw my hands in the air and said, "Okay! I'll meet you there." Bill said, "I'll pick you up at your house."

I don't remember the message preached that evening, but thanks to Bill's persistent concern, I heard the greatest invitation to come. I had heard those words many times, but that night I responded. It was as if God was speaking directly to me. He lovingly called me to come and experience abundant life. On July 7, 1970, I accepted the most important invitation of my life. I came to Him.

Why would anyone turn down a relationship that offers peace, joy, and a purpose to live? Perhaps you don't understand the invitation, or the One who gives it.

THE MISUNDERSTOOD INVITATION

In 1981, I attended a conference on evangelism in Kansas City, Missouri. While I was eating breakfast one morning in a downtown restaurant with several friends, one of them told a story, and I laughed until I cried. He told us about his first train ride as a teenager. He was going to a 4-H conference in Chicago. His parents bought him a first-class ticket from Atlanta to Chicago. The ticket included a reserved seat, reservations in the dining car, and a small single bed in the sleeper car. The conductor showed him onto the train and to the sleeping car to store his luggage. He left the boy at the car, assuming that he understood the privileges of a first-class ticket.

For almost three hours, he sat in his bunk wondering why everyone claimed that first-class train rides were so special. Rather than enjoying the leisure and comfort of the first-class seat that had been purchased for him, he was confined to a single bed on the bottom bunk. He even missed the elaborate meal served in the dining car.

My friend said that evidently word traveled around the train that a guy was sitting fully clothed on a bunk bed. People began walking by his compartment to see the strange sight. Eventually the conductor came to his rescue and explained what his first-class ticket included. Many people who have accepted God's invitation to come to Him do not fully understand what God has purchased for them.

When we respond to God's invitation, what do we receive? Some people are confused about the privileges of journeying through life with God. They believe God puts them in spiritual bondage. They picture a cruel dictator who doesn't want them to experience personal freedom or enjoyment. But nothing could be farther from the truth! God is the One who sets us free from spiritual and psychological oppression. "You will know the truth, and the truth will set you free," Jesus assured the new believers (John 8:32).

The Bible says we have a spiritual enemy, Satan. He was an angel who led a rebellion in heaven and was eternally cast away by God. Satan is the embodiment of evil and destruction. Because God has given His creation free will, we can choose to listen to and believe Satan's lies. Satan's purpose is to take from us, to leave us in a state of constant spiritual turmoil, and eventually to consume our very lives. Jesus referred to Satan as a thief when He said, "The thief comes only to steal and kill and destroy" (John 10:10).

God wants your life to have meaning, purpose, and direction. God cared enough about you to send His only Son into the world. Jesus is the perfect revelation of His Father and the model of loving devotion to God. Jesus ministered through the trauma and temptations of life, ultimately giving His life for our spiritual peace. His victorious life, crucifixion, and resurrection from the dead demonstrate God's loving desire to fellowship with us. Jesus sacrificed Himself so that anyone could come to the Father. What a plan! What an invitation!

CONSIDERING THE INVITATION

We are not the only generation that has struggled with God's invitation. Jesus often spoke with a group of prominent religious leaders who had misconceptions about God. Such misunderstandings about who God is and what He is like are nothing new. The religious leaders of Jesus' lifetime had developed a system of good works. If you kept the rules, God would accept you. If you broke the rules, God would get you! The same system is often used today. Jesus confronted this warped perspective with a story:

> A certain man was preparing a great banquet and invited many guests. At the time of the banquet he sent his servant to tell those who had been invited, "Come, for everything is now

ready." But they all alike began to make excuses. The first said, "I have just bought a field, and I must go and see it. Please excuse me." Another said, "I have just bought five yoke of oxen, and I'm on my way to try them out. Please excuse me." Still another said, "I just got married, so I can't come." The servant came back and reported this to his master. Then the owner of the house became angry and ordered his servant, "Go out quickly into the streets and alleys of the town and bring in the poor, the crippled, the blind and the lame." "Sir," the servant said, "what you ordered has been done, but there is still room." Then the master told his servant, "Go out to the roads and country lanes and make them come in, so that my house will be full. I tell you, not one of those men who were invited will get a taste of my banquet." (Luke 14:16–24)

In this parable, all of the intended guests made excuses to decline the master's invitation. Some probably thought, *I will not be missed.* Perhaps they didn't think the banquet would be fun. Others might have misunderstood the invitation. For whatever reason, taking care of their personal plans was more important than accepting the invitation.

YOUR RESPONSE TO GOD'S INVITATION

I remember the first time I received an invitation to the National Prayer Breakfast. I stared at the elegant white card in my hand. The seal of the United States of America was embossed in gold on the cover. I opened the invitation and read, "You are invited to join the President of the United States of America, the First Lady, the Vice President, the Senate, the House of Representatives, the Supreme Court, the Joint Chiefs of Staff, and other national leaders for prayer." Needless to say, I was proud of my invitation. I kept it on my desk and showed it to friends. I changed my schedule so that I could attend the prayer breakfast.

An invitation to join the government in Washington is exciting, but it isn't comparable to receiving an invitation from God. People have described accepting God's invitation in various ways. One compared it to finding a great treasure. Another said it was the pearl of great price. The scholar C. S. Lewis wrote, "I was surprised by joy."

Those men and women found the true fulfillment, contentment, and significance that come only from God. Of course, you can gain fame without God. We can easily name people who have found wealth and power outside a relationship with Christ. You can also experience pleasure in this life without knowing God. The magazine racks across America are filled with reports of corporate executives, entertainers, and politicians living for self-gratification and rejecting a relationship with God. You can live your entire life ignoring God or blatantly opposing His will. But you cannot experience a life with eternal meaning, true purpose, or clear direction until you respond to God's invitation: "Come."

Use your imagination for a moment. You are sorting through the day's mail one afternoon when you see a formal envelope addressed to you. You curiously open the envelope and pull out a card.

It is an invitation, but you hardly believe that it is not a joke. The card invites you to spend a day at the North Carolina home of Dr. Billy Graham and his family. Dr. Graham has even signed the card.

How can this be? you wonder. You have seen Billy Graham on television, and grown up hearing about him. You have even read one of his books, but you never imagined that you would meet him. He is an internationally-known man of God. He counsels the presidents and speaks to crowds of hundreds of thousands.

You are sure that there must be some mistake but decide to call the RSVP number just in case.

To your amazement, a receptionist at the Billy Graham Evangelical Association headquarters answers your call. You hesitantly give your name, and she warmly responds, "Oh, yes. Dr. Graham has been expecting your call. Will you be able to join the Graham family for the day? They are looking forward to meeting you."

Can I venture a guess at what your response will be? No matter what your denomination or theological persuasion, you will say, "Tell Dr. Graham I'll be there."

Let's stop pretending. Today in reality, you hold in your hands an invitation that is far more important than one stamped by the presidential seal. That invitation could be lost or damaged or canceled because of the president's schedule. The real invitation you hold in your hands is guaranteed. It will never be canceled. You do not have to be concerned about the Lord's travel plans. He is waiting to commune with you twenty-four hours a day from now throughout eternity.

The most important question in all of life is this: Have you accepted God's invitation? He desires that you live in relationship with Him. Why do so many people decline the call of the living God? Take a few moments to list some excuses that people make in our culture to reject God's invitation. Doing this may help you to understand your own response and the response of others. These are some of the reasons people tell me they will not respond to God's call:

- My work keeps me too busy.

- I would need to give up _____.

- My relationships with my family members will be affected; they won't like it.

- What will my friends think? (Pride!)

If you haven't made a decision, here's a closer look at the invitation.

"COME!"—THE OPEN INVITATION

A young man from my church called one evening. "I really need to talk to you," he said. "I know it's late, but I need to work through a bad situation. Is there any way you could meet me tonight?"

"Yes," I said. "Come." My invitation was proof of our friendship.

God's invitation is proof of His love for you. It's a love that responds to your urgency, a love made available at any time and in any situation. God's love desires to help you now in spite of your circumstances.

A miraculous incident in the Bible illustrates the responsiveness of God's love. Jesus' first followers were a group of fishermen. One night, they were out on a lake when a terrible storm arose. Jesus was praying on a nearby mountain. When He saw the crisis on the lake below, He came down from the mountain, across the shore, and walked toward them on the stormy waves.

When Jesus called to the helpless men, Peter yelled from the boat, "'Lord, if it's You . . . tell me to come to You on the water.'

'Come,' He said. Then Peter got down out of the boat, walked on the water and came toward Jesus." (Matt. 14:28–29).

It's a beautiful scene: Jesus, the Son of God, saw the difficulty of someone in need and moved toward him. As the condition grew worse, He moved to greater lengths to meet the obvious need. When Peter recognized Jesus in the storm, he immediately knew that help was available. Then, he did two things that meant the difference between life and death.

First, he responded to Jesus. It wasn't exactly a cry of great faith because Peter said, "Lord, *if* it's You." Yet God meets us where we are. His invitation isn't to some higher level of consciousness. God has made Himself available to meet our deepest personal and spiritual needs. The desire of God's heart is to meet your need. The writer of Hebrews explained that anyone who comes to Him must believe that He exists and that He rewards those who earnestly seek Him (Heb. 11:6).

Second, Peter moved toward Jesus. It wasn't a comfortable journey. People don't usually walk on water! But Peter knew that if he was going to be delivered, he must take that step outside his comfort zone, despite the obstacles. After all, God rewards those who *earnestly* seek Him.

Peter responded to Christ's invitation and experienced a miracle. He "got down out of the boat, walked on the water and came toward Jesus." But more important, Peter was delivered from a deadly situation.

To your hopeless situation, Jesus responds immediately:

- "Come from your crisis to My courage."

- "Come from your longing to My fulfillment."

- "Come from your guilt to My forgiveness."

God invites you to step out and walk toward Him. He'll do the rest!

"COME AS YOU ARE"

Have you received a phone call from friends inviting you to a spontaneous picnic or get-together? If you've been working around the house or relaxing, you probably say, "Well, I need time to change clothes, and what should I bring?" "Oh, just come as you are," they respond. There's no need to dress up or buy two liters of Cola and some chips. Frankly, you don't need to impress anyone. Your friends just want you to come as you are.

Jesus once rebuked those who were more concerned about the way people looked than about their spiritual needs. In response to their superficial outlook, Jesus gave one of the most incredible invitations ever recorded: "Come to Me, all you who are weary and burdened, and I will give you rest" (Matt. 11:28).

"Come just as you are," He was saying. You don't have to meet any requirements first. You can be at your lowest point. Simply bring a heart that longs to have its burden lifted. God invites the weary-hearted and the heavy-laden. He invites everyone with a need.

In Luke's account of the master's banquet, the guests refused the invitations because of their "needs" to satisfy the social and financial requirements of their culture—land, relationships, and careers. Having refused the invitation, those who made excuses were left out. The poor and disabled who came to the party were sorely aware of their needs. They had nothing to offer. But in that state of brokenness, they understood that fellowship and fulfillment are more important than personal agendas. Dropping all pretenses, they responded just as they were.

On another occasion, Jesus gave the invitation, "If anyone is thirsty, let him come to Me and drink" (John 7:37). It's an open invitation. God offers spiritual food and refreshment. Simply come.

"COME HERE!"

Often, the invitation "Come here!" provides guidance or protection. "Come here!" is said for a purpose. It's the same in our relationship with God. He calls us from our foolish rebellion to His infinite wisdom, from a place of danger to His protection. God calls us to a high and holy purpose—the "full" life.

That purpose was evident when Jesus called Peter and his brother, Andrew, to be disciples. "Come, follow Me," Jesus said, "and I will make you fishers of men" (Matt. 4:19). As fishermen, they had a noble profession. In the economy of Galilee, fishing was important. But Jesus wanted to add a greater dimension to their lives. He wanted the brothers to use their skills in work that would have an eternal impact—far beyond their own lives.

Your invitation to "come here" is a call directly from God. Only in Him will you find a life of fulfillment: "I know the plans I have for you," declares the Lord, "plans to prosper you and not to harm you, plans to give you hope and a future" (Jer. 29:11).

"COME ALONE"

This is not a group decision. Jesus is calling you as an individual to accept His personal invitation. Parents or grandparents can't choose for you. The most well-meaning siblings, children, and friends can never respond on your behalf. Not even your pastor or spouse can make this choice. You must "come alone" because this is a personal decision.

Jesus asked the disciples to, "Come with Me by yourselves to a quiet place and get some rest" (Mark 6:31). Each disciple faced a personal choice. He would either answer the Lord's invitation, finding rest, or follow the crowd's festivities, still lacking inner peace. Your encounter with the living God is a personal encounter.

"COME NOW!"

Thanksgiving dinner at my wife's home in Pennsylvania is wonderful. The dinner table stretches through the kitchen and into the living room. For hours, everyone in the house savors the sweet aroma of roasting turkey. By the time dinner is ready, the table is heavy with steaming mashed potatoes, homegrown vegetables, and warm bread. Finally the long-awaited words are spoken. "Dinner's ready!" Grandma calls.

Similar words are used in the Bible as God says, "Come, for everything is now ready" (Luke 14:17). As Grandma returns to the table with the last dish, we gather around the table with family and friends anticipating the food and fellowship we are about to enjoy. This meal has been prepared with love and care, and Grandma wants our families to enjoy the meal she has prepared. If we choose to keep talking or watching the football game, it would be our loss. She has called us to come, and any delay will be lost enjoyment.

God's invitation is for now. He doesn't want you to put off the enjoyment of a living relationship with Him—His forgiveness, healing, deliverance, and much more.

This urgency was obvious during the earthly ministry of Jesus Christ. One day as He was teaching, Jesus spotted a curious observer watching from a tree. The man had climbed the tree because he was too short to see Jesus in the crowd. Jesus understood the hunger in this persistent man's heart. He responded with an invitation: "Zacchaeus, come down immediately. I must stay at your house today" (Luke 19:5). "Come today!" All things are ready; dinner is served.

The Bible culminates with a great invitation: "'Come!' Whoever is thirsty, let him come; and whoever wishes, let him take the free gift of the water of life" (Rev. 22:17). Thirst speaks of a deep need. Water, so essential to our bodies, is like the gift of freedom and love that God offers to fulfill our spiritual needs. How can we truly live without it?

Do you remember the story about the banquet earlier in this chapter? The banquet was made ready, and word was sent out to all the invited guests. "Come, for everything is now ready." But the invited guests made excuses about why they could not come. Do you remember what the master of the banquet said about the people who were invited but chose not to come? "I tell you, not one of those men who were invited will get a taste of my banquet" (Luke 14:24). The point is, your response to God's invitation has eternal consequences. If you reject His invitation to come and you die without knowing Christ as your Lord and Savior, there is no second chance after death.

God has clearly called you. Have you accepted His invitation? I pray you will carefully and prayerfully consider your response. This is absolutely the most important decision you will ever make. Now is the time to deal with your invitation from God.

What do you need to do?

Step 1: God's Purpose: He Wants You to Experience Peace and Eternal Life

God loves you, and He wants you to experience His peace as a way of life.

The Bible says:

- "We have peace with God through our Lord Jesus Christ" (Rom. 5:1).

- "For God so loved the world that He gave His one and only Son, that whoever believes in Him shall not perish but have eternal life" (John 3:16).

- "The gift of God is eternal life in Christ Jesus our Lord" (Rom. 6:23).

It is quite obvious that many people are not enjoying this relationship with God.

Step 2: What's the Problem?: You Are Separated from God by Your Sin

God did not make us robots forced to serve Him. He gave us free will and freedom to choose. Like Adam and Eve, we often choose to disobey God and go our selfish ways. When you disobey God, you sin, and that sin separates you from God.

The Bible says:

- "For all have sinned and fall short of the glory of God . . . [and] . . . the wages of sin is death" (Rom. 3:23; 6:23).

- "Your iniquities have separated you from your God; your sins have hidden His face from you, so that He will not hear" (Isa. 59:2).

Step 3: God's Remedy: The Cross

Jesus Christ is the only answer to the problem of separation from God. He died on the cross and rose from the dead to pay the penalty your sin requires. It has been paid in full! Through

Christ's death and resurrection, Jesus has bridged the gap that separated you from God.

The Bible says:

- "God demonstrates His own love for us in this: While we were still sinners, Christ died for us" (Rom. 5:8).

- "Salvation is found in no one else, for there is no other name under heaven given to men by which we must be saved" (Acts 4:12).

- "For there is one God and one Mediator between God and men, the Man Christ Jesus" (1 Tim. 2:5 NKJV).

- "I tell you the truth, whoever hears My Word and believes Him who sent Me has eternal life and will not be condemned; he has crossed over from death to life" (John 5:24).

God has provided the only way to heaven. You must make the choice.

Step 4: The Answer: Receive Christ

You can receive Christ as your Savior and Lord when you believe in His Word and trust in only Him to save you.

The Bible says:

- "All the prophets testify about Him [Jesus Christ] that everyone who believes in Him receives forgiveness of sins through His name" (Acts 10:43).

- "[Jesus said,] 'Do not let your hearts be troubled. Trust in God; trust also in Me'" (John 14:1).

- "To all who received Him, to those who believed in His name, He gave the right to become children of God" (John 1:12).

How Do You Receive Christ?

1. Admit you are a sinner.

2. Be willing to turn from your sin. (Repent.)

3. Believe that Jesus Christ died for you on the cross as the sacrifice, covering all your sins, and rose from the grave, defeating Satan and death.

4. Through prayer, invite Jesus Christ to come in and control your life through the Holy Spirit. (Receive Him as your Savior.)

What Do You Pray?

Dear Lord Jesus,

I know I am a sinner and I need Your forgiveness. I want to turn from my sin nature and follow You. I believe You died to pay the price for my sin. I invite You to come into my heart and life. Thank You for answering my prayer and for coming into my life. I pray You will help me become a responsible member of Your family.

In Jesus' name I pray. Amen.

3

THE LOVE OF GOD

From Romeo and Juliet to Prince Charles and Princess Diana, romances have captivated our attention throughout history. More people watched the royal wedding of Charles and Diana than any other wedding. It seemed as though the entire world was glued to the television. But how sad to see that fairy-tale romance gradually crumble before the watching world.

Something about a love story attracts attention. Some of the hottest-selling books on the market today are romance novels. Their popularity is another sign that deep down inside, all of us desire to experience love. And if we can't experience it, at least we can read about it.

Have you ever received a love letter? Love letters are very special because they communicate our heartfelt feelings to someone special. A number of years ago our family was preparing to move to Chicago, where I would go to seminary. I was in the basement of our home sorting through things and packing for our move. In one of the boxes, I found a stack of love letters Barbara had written to me the summer before we were married. Rather than finish the packing, I sat down and started reading. Those letters mean little to anyone else, but I cherish them. Why? They are written personally to me from someone whom I love and who loves me.

I like to think of the Bible as a love letter written personally to me. In reality, it is a personal love letter written from our loving Creator to every man and woman throughout time. It was written especially to you. Think about it for a moment—the God of all creation has communicated His love for you in the Bible. A love letter from God to you!

To be loved by anyone is a wonderful experience. But to know that the God of all creation loves me personally is an awesome thought. It's incomprehensible. The Bible talks a lot about the love of God. It explains that He loves you as an individual. Let's look at what that means.

FACETS OF LOVE

Yes, love is a wonderful experience, but it is difficult to define, especially in the English language. For instance, I love the Lord. I am in love with my wife, Barbara. I love my children, Michelle and David. In a tennis match, my score may be love–15. I even love peanut butter and jelly sandwiches with a glass of milk. You'll agree that these are not similar expressions! Yet in the English language we have only one word to express many different forms of love.

In Greek (the original language of the New Testament), four words are used to express different types of love: *storge, phileo, eros,* and *agape.*

Storge

Storge refers to the love between a parent and a child. I believe that one must be a parent to fully understand this love. I remember the happy anticipation Barbara and I had prior to the birth of our two children, and the overwhelming love I personally felt the moment they were born. I cannot begin to comprehend how God gave up His only Son. In all honesty, I would not be willing to sacrifice the life of either of my children to save someone else. Yet that is how much God loves you; "He gave His one and only Son" for you (John 3:16).

Phileo

Phileo, another Greek word, describes love between two good friends. The older I get, the more I value this aspect of love. One of my top three goals in life is to have at least twelve close friends who will sit through my funeral service without looking at their watches. Consider making it one of your goals too. An essential aspect of life is friendship. When you die, the things that really matter will be your faith, your family, and your friends. Friendship love is very important. It requires work and commitment but is worth the effort.

I am blessed with many opportunities to practice *phileo*, and I thank God for many good friends. I am especially indebted to several close friends who have helped me become the person I am today. Major transitions have become a part of our modern society. It is not uncommon to move across the country or much farther. I know a family who—in the past fifteen years—has been transferred from Puerto Rico to the Philippines, back to Puerto Rico, and recently to Texas. Each move has offered each family member wonderful opportunities, and they have handled the transitions well as a family. But a challenge has been leaving behind good friends. God has been faithful to this family, providing new friends and a good church family after each move. But *phileo* takes time to build.

Today's world often replaces the *phileo* so adequately described in the Greek with superficial status or self-serving "friendships." I am thankful to have two older friends who have modeled for me the importance of being a loyal friend. Both Amos and John are old enough to be my father. They have modeled for others a well-lived life. Their commitment to their faith in God, their loving commitment to family, and their loyalty as friends during good times and bad portray true friendship. I am grateful to Amos and John for their example and friendship.

Another great model of this kind of love has been my father-in-law. He has been part of the "hunting gang" for more than fifty years. The sixteen men have shared a hunting cabin in the mountains of Pennsylvania, and they meet there a few times each year to enjoy family vacations, snowmobile, hunt deer, or fish. Last year they celebrated fifty years of friendship with a week-long bus trip together with their wives.

I often ask myself, *Am I working to develop that kind of friendship?* Whether you've just moved to a new city or you're beginning retirement, take time to cherish and cultivate friendship love.

Eros

Eros is strong passion. The English word *erotic* comes from the Greek *eros*. So often, the world abuses and cheapens the gifts God created for good. God designed this type of love to be experienced between a husband and a wife where *eros* brings fulfillment, joy, and pleasure.

God has blessed me with a loving wife. Barbara and I have been married for more than twenty-five years. I love her more today than the day I married her. I am thankful to God for the privilege of sharing passionate love with Barbara. There is absolutely nothing cheap or dirty about this kind of love. It is a gift of God intended to be shared between a husband and a wife.

This type of love can be fully experienced and appreciated only within the freedom of a marriage commitment. When someone tries to experience this type of love outside a marriage relationship, it results in guilt, pain, and lack of fulfillment. Of course, there is an immediate feeling of pleasure from the sex act itself, but real *eros* love is intended to bring far more pleasure than immediate sexual pleasure. God created *eros* for good, and He wants everyone who is called to a life of marriage to enjoy it to the full within the bounds of marriage.

Obviously God did not call everyone to marry. If He has called you to a life of singleness, you will not experience *eros*. For the men and women God calls to singleness, He will meet your every need. Our modern culture may make you feel less than normal. But as I understand the Bible, God regards singleness as a high calling.

Agape

Agape, the fourth Greek word for love, focuses on the person who is doing the loving more than on the one being loved. It especially connotes action, doing something for the other person. God demonstrated this type of love for all of us when "He gave His one and only Son, that whoever believes in Him shall not perish but have eternal life" (John 3:16).

All four aspects of love are gifts from God. Yes, many people have abused and misunderstood each type of love. But God created each form of love and gave it to us to enjoy.

I have always been loved, for which I am humbly thankful to God. Growing up, I received encouragement, affirmation, and love. Today, I enjoy a fulfilling and growing marriage with my wife, Barbara. We love each other. I also have a fun and loving relationship with my two children. Together, our family members have made a habit of verbally affirming our love. "I love you," I remind them before I hang up the phone or leave for a breakfast meeting.

Perhaps your experience with love is totally different from mine. You may know the pain of rejection and abuse. Even as you read this chapter, you wonder if the hurts will ever disappear: *Will anyone accept me and love me for who I am?* For you, I believe there is hope. In fact, you are already loved, and you can experience the joy of unconditional love today.

GOD'S LOVE LETTER

Did you know that the Bible is a declaration of God's love? Yes, it records a lot of historical facts, but the primary message of the Bible is to tell you and all humanity that God loves you.

Our world is full of ardent declarations of love. Billboards, license plates, and diamond rings are used to express romantic love. When I think of Christ's unequaled sacrificial love, I am often reminded of a story I heard during the Vietnam War. An orphanage had been bombed, and several of the orphan boys were injured. A field hospital was set up to perform surgery. One child was in desperate need of a blood transfusion. Nurses found a young boy with the same blood type. In broken Vietnamese, a nurse tried to explain his friend's emergency need to the boy. "If your friend does not receive blood, he will die," the nurse said. The little boy agreed to donate blood for his injured friend. He lay quietly on the table as the nurse took his blood pressure and prepared the needle and bag. When the needle was inserted and his blood began running into the bag hanging below the table, the boy began to cry. He looked up to a Vietnamese worker and asked, "Mister, when do I die?"

The child believed that by donating his blood, he was giving up his life for his friend. That is true love! I am sure everyone would like to have such a friend. The Bible speaks of this kind of love: "Very rarely will anyone die for a righteous man, though for a good man someone might possibly dare to die. But God demonstrates His own love for us in this: While we were still sinners, Christ died for us" (Rom. 5:7–8).

Did you realize that God's love is declared more than nineteen hundred times in the Bible? That's emphatic! Clearly God has a message: He loves us.

The New Testament is filled with references to the love of God: "Whoever does not love does not know God, because God is love . . . This is love: not that we loved God, but that He loved us" (1 John 4:8, 10); "greater love has no man than to lay down his life for his friends" (John 15:13 NKJV); "By this we know love, because He first loved us. And we ought also to lay down our lives for the brethren" (1 John 3:16 NKJV). These verses make clear the message of the Bible: "God loves you."

DEFINING GOD'S LOVE

In the midst of their rock stardom, the Beatles sang of love "eight days a week"! People are always striving for a newer, better way to say, "I love you." I think the apostle Paul felt the same limitations when he was writing his letter to the church in Ephesus. He wrote, "I pray that you, being rooted and established in love, may have power, together with all the saints, to grasp how wide and long and high and deep is the love of Christ, and to know this love that surpasses knowledge" (Eph. 3:17–19).

Notice that in verse 19, he said the love of God surpasses all *knowledge*. In other words, no one has the ability to comprehend everything about God's love. No one can define the love of God. If you could define God, one of two things would be true. You would be God (excuse me for saying so, but that is a frightening thought). Or the god you define would not be God. Either way we would be in trouble. The extent of God and His love for us is unfathomable and indefinable, but His Word describes this love in several helpful analogies. Paul prayed that we "may have power . . . to grasp how wide and long and high and deep is the love of Christ" (Eph. 3:18).

How Wide Is God's Love?

One expression of God's love is His infinite forgiveness of our sins. David wrote, "As far as the east is from the west, so far has He removed our transgressions from us" (Ps. 103:12). That is a measureless distance. God did not say He would remove our sins as far as the north is from the south. You can measure that distance. The North Pole is a single point in the Arctic where all the earth's longitudinal lines meet. U.S. explorer Robert Peary reached that point by dogsled almost a century ago. A permanent scientific base was established in 1956 at the South Pole in Antarctica. But no one has ever reached the "East Pole" or "West Pole". Regardless of how far eastward you travel, you're still going east. Regardless of how far westward you go, you're still going west. God said He would remove our sin "as far as the east is from the west," an infinite distance. God's eternal forgiveness reflects His love: it is boundless.

We can remember when we have sinned. But God chooses not only to forgive our sin, but also to forget our sin. Once you have asked God to forgive your sin, He forgives and He forgets. I once heard Holocaust survivor Corrie ten Boom say, "God buries our sin in the depth of the ocean of His love and puts up a 'No Fishing' sign." Have you experienced His forgiving love?

How Long Is God's Love?

"If I leave my wife and family for another woman, will God still love me?" a middle-aged man asked me one afternoon in my office. I have heard similar questions many times before. You may be struggling with the possibility of adultery, premarital sex, deception in business practices, or tax fraud. These are all sins, but by no means the only sins.

If you choose to sin, does God still love you? God does not love you based on what you do or don't do. God is love! Period. There is nothing you can ever do that will change His love for you. God declared, "I have loved you with an everlasting love; therefore with lovingkindness I have drawn you" (Jer. 31:3 NKJV). He will always love you with His "everlasting love." God grieves when we do not live in relationship with Him, but He always loves us. God's love never slows down or runs out. Regardless of how far away from God you may be, His "everlasting love" reaches out to you. He desires to draw everyone into relationship with Him.

Of course, I must be honest with you about the consequences of bad choices. Even though God will always love us, regardless of our actions or attitudes, we often pay a terrible price for making wrong choices. The Bible says, "The wages of sin is death" (Rom. 6:23 NKJV). Sin really does have a high price tag. The Bible acknowledges that there are "pleasures of sin for a short time" (Heb. 11:25), but it also gives the rest of the story: "Do not be deceived, God is not mocked; for whatever a man sows, that he will also reap" (Gal. 6:7 NKJV). Yes, you will probably pay a huge price for wrong choices, but the fact remains: God loves you.

How High Is God's Love?

We are a space-conscious society. We have watched men walk on the moon and heard NASA's plans to visit Mars. We're accustomed to people circling Earth. Powerful telescopes explore our universe and beyond. Our television programs and telephone connections are beamed from satellites floating in space. Astronomers say that Venus, the planet closest to Earth, is twenty-five million miles away at its closest approach. Alpha Centauri is a star system 4.3 light-years away that is approaching our system at fourteen miles per second. I cannot comprehend such distance in such a massive universe.

I remember when the first Russian circled Earth in a spaceship. After he returned to Earth following his mission, he announced he had been into the heavens and did not see God. I always wanted to tell him that if he had jumped out of his spaceship, he certainly would have met God!

But seriously, if we could ascend beyond this entire massive universe to the throne of God, we would see a God who longs for us to live in an intimate relationship with Him. The Bible teaches us that not even a sparrow falls to the ground without His awareness (Matt. 10:29). If God is conscious of a sparrow, how much more are you—a person—on His mind? The height of His love reaches from the lowest parts of this universe to the very throne room of God. Pause for a moment and meditate on the height of His love for you. It is an awesome thought to realize that the God of all creation is sitting in the throne room of heaven thinking about you as an individual. That is the measure of the height of His love.

How Deep Is God's Love?

Jack Murphy was an unusually talented and brilliant young man. While attending the University of Pennsylvania on a full scholarship, he became the youngest first-chair violinist in the history of the Pittsburgh Symphony Orchestra. He left college to join the Barnum and Bailey Circus as a stunt diver. His act required him to dive one hundred feet into a small tub of water. Soon he left the circus and became a surfing champion. In surfing circles, he is still known as Murph the Surf, and he holds the record for hurricane surfing. Then Jack committed the largest jewel theft in history. He was captured, and after three years in prison, he was released. But instead of learning from his mistakes, the gifted young man committed a terrible crime, and he received two life sentences plus twenty years.

A chaplain visited Jack and told him of God's love. Jack was incredulous and said, "No way! How can God love me? I have two life sentences plus twenty years. Don't tell me God loves me." The chaplain returned week after week, and finally Jack Murphy opened his heart and experienced the joy of forgiveness through Jesus Christ. Through a series of miracles, he was later released from prison and is now in full-time prison ministry. Jack tells hurting men and women firsthand of Christ's love.

A life such as Jack Murphy's exemplifies the depth of God's unconditional love. Even when we trash the most incredible gifts God has given us and completely reject Him, God longs for us to return to Him. He still loves us. I meet many people who think they have done so many bad things, God could never love them or forgive them. But don't limit God! His love reaches deeper than any guilt you are struggling with.

Guilt is one of the greatest problems of our world. Overwhelmed by a sense of their wrongs, people develop ulcers; guilt sours relationships with suspicion and competition and sends many into deep depression. Dr. Joseph M. Stowell claims that the hopelessness that has made suicide the second leading cause of death among youth stems from two problems everyone faces: fear and guilt. Yes, guilt is something all humans long to be released from, even through "guilt-free" desserts and luxuries we "deserve." The good news is, there is a remedy to guilt! We don't have to live with the misery of past failures. Consider Paul's comment in 1 Timothy 1:15: "Here is a trustworthy saying that deserves full acceptance: Christ Jesus came into the world to save sinners—of whom I am the worst." John explained, "This is love: not that we loved God, but that He first loved us and sent His Son as an atoning sacrifice for our sins" (1 John 4:10). "From within, out of men's hearts, come evil thoughts, sexual immorality, theft, murder, adultery, greed, malice, deceit, lewdness, envy, slander, arrogance and folly. All these evils come from inside and make a man 'unclean'" (Mark 7:21–23). But the love of God goes deeper than any sin.

GOD'S ULTIMATE SYMBOL OF LOVE

Did you know that the cross is really a symbol of God's love? In our society, it is often a meaningless piece of jewelry or an archaic relic. But the cross should always remind us of God's unconditional and sacrificial love for each of us. Jesus took all of our sins on Himself when He died on the cross. Although He had never done wrong, He chose to accept God's punishment for us. Because God is holy, He cannot interact with us as long as we are tainted by sin. In the Old Testament, God made a way for the Israelites to be cleansed of their sins through the symbolic sacrifice of an animal.

God remains the same today—He is holy and cannot tolerate our personal sins. But today, our sins can be covered by the ultimate sacrifice Jesus made almost two thousand years ago. By giving up Himself as the perfect Son of God, Jesus' blood covers our sins when we put our faith in Him. Second Corinthians 5:21

points out that "God made Him [Jesus] who had no sin to be sin for us, so that in Him we might become the righteousness of God." First Peter 2:24 explains that Christ "Himself bore our sins in His body on the tree, so that we might die to sins and live for righteousness; by His wounds you have been healed."

The cross of Christ is the ultimate symbol of God's love. If we could stand before the cross and view the Son of almighty God dying for our sins, we would begin to understand the height, depth, length, and width of the love of God.

Visit that awful scene in your imagination. Imagine looking up to see your loving and all-powerful God bleeding on that cross and dying in your place—Christ, who never sinned, dying for every one of your sins. There's a crown of thorns pressed on the head of the One who knew you even before He formed you in your mother's womb (Jer. 1:5). Look up on the cross, just above Christ's bleeding head. The Roman soldiers hung a sign there to ridicule Christ. "King of the Jews," it said. In your imagination, write "the height of God's love" above that sign.

Now, kneel down to Jesus' nail-pierced feet. Those feet walked the dusty and dirty streets of Galilee. But they never walked in sin. Christ is the Master of the universe, the King of kings, and the Lord of lords. "He is before all things, and in Him all things hold together," declares Colossians 1:17. He is the Author and Sustainer of life itself. He is the Creator who knows your thoughts before you speak them (Ps. 139:4).

God created the human race to live in fellowship with Him, but sin broke that holy relationship. The very world He endowed with free will rejected His love and chose to live in sin. But God loves you and me so much that He left the glory of heaven to be born into this world. God came to earth, taking on human flesh. The King of all creation became a human being. He was born into poverty and lived a life of rejection. To pay the price for sin with His sinless blood, He died on the cross. Kneel down below His nail-pierced feet and write "the depth of God's love."

As you face the God of all creation dying on the cross, see His right hand nailed to the cross and stiffened in pain. That hand calmed the sea and fed the hungry. His hand healed the sick and raised the dead. He welcomed little children into His presence and invited the most scandalous sinners to come and eat with Him. Beside His right hand, write "the length of God's love."

Stand by His left side, where the very heart of God is broken, bleeding, and dying for you. Beside the nail-pierced hand, write "the width of God's love."

I cannot begin to comprehend the significance of each of these symbols of love and sacrifice. But I know that the cross of Christ is God's ultimate declaration of love. The Romans did not really take His life. Neither did the Jews. As He had proved throughout his life, Jesus had the supernatural power to come down from the cross at any moment. Instead, He chose to give His perfect, sinless life to cover your sins so that you can experience a life of love and relationship with God.

No one can give a complete definition of the love of God, but we find His love on almost every page of the Bible, His love letter to us. No matter what your experience has been with earthly loves, God's love is here for you today and always. It's as wide as His infinite forgiveness. It lasts forever. It will never change. God's love for you reaches up to His throne in heaven and deeper than your darkest sin. His unconditional, indescribable love is best expressed in His sacrifice on the cross.

Take time to meditate on these hymns:

"When I Survey the Wondrous Cross"
by ISAAC WATTS

When I survey the wondrous cross
On which the Prince of glory died,
My richest gain I count but loss,
And pour contempt on all my pride.

Forbid it, Lord, that I should boast,
Save in the death of Christ my God;
All the vain things that charm me most,
I sacrifice them to His blood.

See, from His head, His hands, His feet,
Sorrow and love flow mingled down;
Did e'er such love and sorrow meet,
Or thorns compose so rich a crown?

Were the whole realm of nature mine,
That were an offering far too small;
Love so amazing, so divine,
Demands my soul, my life, my all.

"The Love of God"
by F. M. LEHMANSBY

The love of God is greater far than tongue or pen can ever tell;
It goes beyond the highest star, and reaches to the lowest hell.
The guilty pair, bowed down with care, God gave His Son to win,
His erring child He reconciled, and pardoned from his sin.

Chorus
O love of God, how rich and pure!
How measureless and strong!
It shall forever more endure the saints and angels' song.

When years of time shall pass away, and earthly thrones and
    kingdoms fall;
When men, who here refuse to pray, on rocks and hills and
    mountains call;
God's love, so sure, shall still endure, all measureless and
    strong;
Redeeming grace to Adam's race—the saints' and angels' song.

Could we with ink the ocean fill and were the skies of parch-
    ment made;
Were every stalk on earth a quill, and every man a scribe by
    trade;
To write the love of God above, would drain the ocean dry.
Nor could the scroll contain the whole, though stretched from
    sky to sky.

4

THE JOY OF FORGIVENESS

Have you ever thought about what God looks like? Or wondered about His personality? I love to tell the story about a boy who was asked to draw a picture in his kindergarten class. His teacher walked through the room, looking at the students' artwork. When she stopped at Billy's desk, she asked him what he was drawing. "I'm drawing a picture of God," Billy answered. "But, Billy, no one knows what God looks like!" the teacher said. "They will when I'm finished," Billy said.

If someone asked you to draw a picture of God today, what would He look like?

PICTURING GOD

There are many misconceptions about who God is and what He is like. Some people see God as a "holy janitor." People with this perception live for self-gratification, doing their own thing, never considering God. But inevitably even the most self-sufficient person ends up in a huge mess. Then the questions begin: *Why would God let this happen to me? Do I deserve this?* Often they scream for help. They scream for God, the holy janitor, to report immediately and clean up the mess. Often they promise, "Lord,

I promise to do better;" "I promise I will start going to church;" or "I will *never* do this again if You will help me."

Others see God as a holy bellhop. They struggle through life, carrying burdens until the load is so heavy, they can't take another step. They call out for God to help them *now!* But they never learn to trust God with the cares of their lives. As soon as they regain their personal strength, they pick up the burdens again and struggle on—starting the cycle again.

A destructive misconception of God is the mean father image. Maybe you have also seen God as mean and hurtful. God is somewhere upstairs in heaven watching your every move, waiting for you to mess up so He can zap you. I'm sad to say that this is one of the most prominent views of God today. Many people associate their memories of less-than-perfect earthly fathers with God. Perhaps your dad abused you physically or emotionally. The temptation is to transfer the dread, fear, hurt, and disappointment you feel toward your earthly father to God.

I pray that I can convey the true nature of God to you. God is a loving Father who longs to live in relationship with you. The Bible tells us, "God demonstrates His own love toward us, in that while we were still sinners, Christ died for us" (Rom. 5:8 NKJV). He longs to accept you and forgive you for every wrong you've ever done. The strategy that secures your forgiveness is God's idea. He initiated the plan because He wants to be your loving heavenly Father.

PRACTICING FORGIVENESS

A man who had survived the Holocaust was a leader of the Warsaw ghetto uprising. He spoke of the bitterness that remains in his soul over the persecution he and his neighbors endured under the Nazis. "If you could lick my heart," he says, "it would poison you." This man's honesty is the reality of too many people in our world.

Do you harbor bitterness because you have failed to practice forgiveness? Too many of us choose to live with unforgiveness. But this choice hinders your relationship with God, and it hinders your interactions with people. Bitterness that swells up under your refusal to forgive will ultimately destroy the joy of life. It can control you to such an extent that it destroys your most important relationships. It can also destroy you.

Have you ever prayed the Lord's Prayer? Do you remember what you prayed? "Forgive us our debts (or trespasses), as we also have forgiven our debtors (or those who trespass against us)." In simple terms, "God, forgive me in the same way that I forgive those who hurt me." Did you realize that you prayed that to almighty God?

Being forgiving is a vital way of life. Being unforgiving will affect your physical well-being in this life and your eternal destiny. Even secular psychologists are recognizing the importance of the Christian virtue of forgiveness.

Barbara and I have been married for more than twenty-five years, and I believe we have a wonderful marriage. Yet during our years together, I sometimes have had to go to Barbara and ask, "Will you forgive me?" As I look back on our marriage, I'm thankful for the advice that my mom gave us prior to our wedding. Barbara and I had read great books to prepare for married life. We went to counseling sessions offered by our college to engaged couples. Despite all that, I believe the greatest advice we received was my mom's reminder, "Do not let the sun go down while you are still angry" (Eph. 4:26).

Of course, no one likes to admit being wrong. I'm tempted

to play mind games: "If I ignore the situation, maybe it will go away." Or I may assure myself that Barbara needs to ask me to forgive her: "After all, it wasn't really my fault!"

The best advice is, it is always my move. If everyone practiced this principle, think of all the broken relationships that could be healed. Unresolved anger and a checklist of past wrongs will fester into major conflict. But forgiveness brings healing and reconciliation. Never delay requesting or extending forgiveness. Do it today before the sun goes down.

There is sweet joy in forgiving and being forgiven. Relationships are not only restored, but they're made stronger, regardless of the disagreement.

Is there someone you need to forgive? You may protest, "If you only knew what that person did to me. He doesn't deserve to be forgiven!" You may be right. He doesn't deserve to be forgiven. Guess what? You don't deserve God's forgiveness, and neither do I. But God was willing to forgive us anyway.

GOD'S FORGIVENESS

Forgiveness at a human level is necessary in every functioning relationship. But we have a deeper need for spiritual forgiveness. Forgiveness from God will give you overwhelming peace, unlike any reconciliation you've ever had.

If you're starting to feel guilty about unreconciled conflicts, you're not alone. We are not the first generation to struggle with forgiveness. It is a problem that plagues our world and has been an obstacle throughout history. The Jewish society of Jesus' time had devised standard systems of forgiveness. One group believed they were so bad, they could never please God; therefore, they saw no need to try. The other group, religious leaders, thought that if they had enough rules, they could please God by being good. The latter audience listened to Jesus' story in Luke 15:11–20.

> There was a man who had two sons. The younger one said to his father, "Father, give me my share of the estate." So he divided his property between them. Not long after that, the younger son got together all he had, set off for a distant country and there squandered his wealth in wild living. After he had spent everything, there was a severe famine in that whole country, and he began to be in need. So he went and hired himself out to a citizen of that country, who sent him to his fields to feed pigs. He longed to fill his stomach with the pods that the pigs were eating, but no one gave him anything. When he came to his senses, he said, "How many of my father's hired men have food to spare, and here I am starving to death! I will set out and go back to my father and say to him: Father, I have sinned against heaven and against you. I am no longer worthy to be called your son; make me like one of your hired men." So he got up and went to his father.

To understand this story, you must learn about its setting.

First, it was unthinkable for a son to ask his father to give him his share of the estate. The son showed complete disrespect for his father. His request was similar to that of a child in our society demanding his share of his parents' will—essentially wishing them dead.

Second, he received his share of the estate, and he took it and left his family without a second glance. He traveled to a foreign country. Family and culture were very important to the Jewish community. When the young man left, he showed no regard for his father, his family, or his people. It was an unforgivable offense as far as the religious leaders were concerned.

Third, he wasted all the money. Again, a good young Jewish man should not act this way. He was to be a good manager of money. Money was not to be wasted; it was to be used wisely and saved.

Fourth, he began as a privileged young Jewish man. He ended up feeding pigs and longing for pig food. Jesus took this story to an entirely different level for the religious leaders listening to Him. To the Jewish community, the scenario was unthinkable. Pigs were considered unclean animals. The young man had sunk as low as anyone in the Jewish community could get. The crowd listening to Jesus' story had almost more than they could handle. From their perspective and within their culture, the father had every right to totally disown his son. The son did not deserve his father's forgiveness.

Jesus painted such a drastically bad picture so that we would begin to understand that it is His nature to forgive. Like the rebellious young man, not one of us deserves to be forgiven. Like the religious leaders listening to Jesus' story, we cannot earn forgiveness. God has chosen to grant His forgiveness through His Son, Jesus Christ, who died on the cross to pay the price for our sins. Forgiveness is a gift from God that is neither earned nor deserved.

But do you realize that the story Jesus told about the prodigal son almost two thousand years ago is really about you and me? All of us have run away from God in our own way. Yes, some of us ran farther away than others, but all of us need His forgiveness.

Maybe you identify more with the older son who stayed home. Maybe you were planning to work your way to heaven on good deeds. Or you might have given up on the whole thing! Still, God is longing for you to come into a relationship with Him today. The group of self-righteous religious leaders who listened to Jesus' story were just as guilty as the young man who ran away with his father's money. No one will ever make it to heaven by being good enough. Even my best "goodness" will never measure up to the expectations of a holy God who is completely without sin. But neither can I run far enough away to escape His presence. The only answer is to return to the One who created me.

Why don't you come home? He is waiting to forgive you!

What do you need to do? Ask Him!

THE LOST SON

The lost son's life is a vivid lesson. How could he descend so quickly from a life of privilege to a life of poverty? What happened in his slide downward that is applicable to our lives?

1. The son began his descent by ignoring what he had and looking for something better: "The younger son got together all he had, set off for a distant country and there squandered his wealth in wild living" (v. 13).

He had the privilege of his father's estate. He had his father's goods, and he had household servants to act upon his every request. The best that his father had to offer him was at his disposal every moment of his life. He was an heir to his father's property, possessions, and prestige. But he traded right living for wild living.

He set his eyes on a "distant country," the other—greener— side of the fence. Not content with what he already had, he longed for something more. It's a familiar trap. "My spouse seems to show less affection. If only . . ." or "I deserved that promotion!

How did she get to be the department supervisor?" Sometimes envy for a competitor's goods ends in robbery. Lust for someone else's partner can end in adultery. And jealousy over a colleague's position results in a bitter rivalry.

Discontent is the father of disobedience. The discontent begins to take root in the heart. Soon we begin to imagine the scenario that would give us what we long for. The next step is acting on our fantasies—a descent into blatant disobedience of God's will for our lives.

2. When he turned his back on his father's best, the son ended up with the world's worst: "After he had spent everything, there was a severe famine in that whole country, and he began to be in need" (v. 14).

The lost son bought the promises of a better country. But his dreams turned into a nightmare. The late humorist Erma Bombeck once titled a bestselling book *The Grass Is Always Greener over the Septic Tank.* That's a fitting description of what those who look for the *better* may find.

Notice the steps: (a) "he had spent everything," and (b) "there was a severe famine." When we turn our backs on the right choices and commit ourselves to something less, life usually gets worse. Instead of fulfillment, we end up with want.

3. His separation from his father changed his status: "So he went and hired himself out to a citizen of that country, who sent him to his fields to feed pigs" (v. 15).

The lost son went from prominence in his father's house to subservience in a stranger's. He no longer commanded the servants; he was one of them. His status changed with his behavior. It usually happens that way. We set our sights away from the good and the right, and we end up as slaves to our choices.

Even his employment was not what he had intended. A man

of his Jewish culture would have nothing to do with pigs. Yet he became a pig keeper. His status changed. Instead of being an owner, he was owned. His talents that had been used in building up his father's estate were merely tools for increasing the wealth of a man who rejected everything he stood for.

4. His outlook changed his disposition from carefree to despairing: "When he came to his senses, he said, 'How many of my father's hired men have food to spare, and here I am starving to death!'" (v. 17).

His new position gave him a brand-new mind-set. He went from daring to see a better country and wasting all his money to living in despair and eating pig food just to stay alive. His freedom turned into bitter bondage.

One of the many causes of depression is the realization of lost opportunity. The lost son was remorseful over what he had left behind, the life he had exchanged for the squalor he experienced. He was depressed. Instead of looking forward, he looked back to the past. He remembered the lifestyle he gave up. He now appreciated the acceptance that he had traded for his present rejection.

He understood his position—and understood that it was inferior to one he previously held. He understood his situation— and understood that he made the personal choices that put him there. He was a victim of his careless decisions. He knew that even his father's hired servants were better off than he was.

You may say, "I know exactly how the lost son feels! I've been there. I've done that." You may be a victim of your own careless decisions. Spiritually you may have turned your back on God's acceptance and provision for a trip to the far country. You dreamed of freedom and the thrill of a better life, and you ended up with it costing far more than you ever dreamed. The cheap thrill has turned out to be very costly. Instead of fulfillment, you feel an ache in your spirit. You have achieved what you thought you wanted, but you find it isn't what you really need. Rather than enjoy freedom, you find yourself in bondage.

I'm glad the story doesn't end in the pigpen. The lost son found his way back home—back to the father. God's Word is a word of hope. It always leads us to a better place. Look at the son's return trip.

THE FOUND SON

Just as he made some decisive steps downward, the lost son in Jesus' story took some decisive steps upward. The lost became found. How?

1. He decided to change directions: "I will set out and go back to my father and say to him: 'Father, I have sinned against heaven and against you'" (v. 18).

He made the decision to leave. He took an honest look at his situation and realized how costly his decision had been. His decision to go to a distant country didn't work. It cost him everything. When we distance ourselves from what we know is right, trouble always follows. The lost son had to change directions in order to be the found son.

How did he decide to change directions? He said, "I have sinned." In other words, "I admit that I am going in the wrong direction." I spend a lot of time traveling to various speaking engagements. I know what it is to be on a road trip to a certain destination and suddenly discover that I don't know where I am— I am lost. How do I finally arrive at the right destination? I admit that I am lost. Unless I make that commitment in my mind, I will never make it to the place that I set out to find. I will just keep going in the wrong direction. (I'll keep living in the "lost mode".)

I may be driving the latest in automobile technology. I may have an onboard navigation system. I may have the best advice of the mapping experts in my hand. But I will never get to the place where I want to be until I admit that I am going in the wrong direction. The son in Jesus' story had to admit he was lost.

I also have to admit the consequence of my wrong direction. If I keep going the wrong way, I'll only be farther away from my destination. If I arrive an hour late for my speaking engagement, I will have failed my commitment, and people will be disappointed. My wrong direction affects others.

The lost son started his journey back by admitting his "lostness" and by admitting its consequence—its effect on others. He said, "Father, I have sinned against heaven and against you." He had not only rejected his father, but also rejected everything his father stood for. He betrayed his father's values as well as his vocation.

2. His attitude changed. The haughty and rebellious spirit of the lost son was transformed. He became contrite. His personality didn't change—his father still recognized his adventurous son. But the son recognized that his rebellious spirit had brought him nothing but heartache and broken dreams: "I am no longer worthy to be called your son; make me like one of your hired men" (v. 19).

His proud, demanding spirit became submissive. He recognized that any restoration his father offered would come from his good graces. In the lost son's mind, the father was again in the driver's seat. His journey from lost son to found son included a change of attitude.

It's an important spiritual truth. When we seek a restored spiritual relationship with God, we recognize who He is—the Lord of creation. Paul, the great apostle of the Lord Jesus Christ, taught this truth in biblical times to the scholars of Athens: "The God who made the world and everything in it is the Lord of heaven and earth and does not live in temples built by hands. And He is not served by human hands, as if He needed anything, because He Himself gives all men life and breath and everything else" (Acts 17:24–25).

3. He "got up and went." Whether it's to the neighbor's house next door or the farthest tip of the continent, every journey begins with the first step. The son began his journey back to the father with a solitary step: "So he got up and went to his father" (v. 20).

He changed his direction, his disposition, and his position. He got up! It shows determination. His stature, once bowed low by his despair, became erect. He straightened his back, lifted his shoulders, set his eyes toward home, and took a step.

Was it a difficult step? Yes! He had been living in a pigpen. He had to swallow his pride and return to his hometown in complete humiliation. But if he was going to get home—back to the pardon and provision of his father—he had to take a stand. He had to abandon his current place to get to a better place.

It was a step of faith. He started home, believing that the arrival would be worth the effort. In our spiritual journey, it's the same: "Without faith it is impossible to please God, because anyone who comes to Him must believe that He exists and that He rewards those who earnestly seek Him" (Heb. 11:6).

4. His reunion was greater than his rebellion. The whole time the son was looking toward home, his father had been watching. And the depth of the reunion was far greater than the breach of his rebellion:

> While he was still a long way off, his father saw him and was filled with compassion for him; he ran to his son, threw his arms around him and kissed him. The son said to him, "Father, I have sinned against heaven and against you. I am no longer

worthy to be called your son." But the father said to his servants, "Quick! Bring the best robe and put it on him. Put a ring on his finger and sandals on his feet. Bring the fattened calf and kill it. Let's have a feast and celebrate. For this son of mine was dead and is alive again; he was lost and is found." So they began to celebrate (Luke 15:20–24).

A WONDERFUL REUNION

Let's notice several points about that wonderful reunion.

The Father Anticipated It

First, the heart of the father anticipated it long before it happened. The father was longing for his son's return. It's the same in our spiritual restoration. Long before we decide to go back to our Creator and heavenly Father, He is looking for us. He wants a healed relationship with us. While we are still far off, He sees us and has compassion toward us. Every preconceived idea about God turns to dust when we meet Him. The Bible says, "The Lord . . . is patient with you, not wanting anyone to perish, but everyone to come to repentance" (2 Peter 3:9).

The Son Kept His Word

Second, the son kept his word. He said he would ask his father to forgive him, and he did. Restoration with God is serious. Lighthearted commitments made in the midst of a traumatic experience or emotional event are usually abandoned over time. Whatever vows we make in our hearts on our return to the Father's house should be made thoughtfully (Deut. 23:21). Our relationship with God is the most important relationship we will ever have.

The father offered acceptance to the son who deserved to be rejected, disowned, and forgotten. The dad was thrilled to see him return. He never mentioned his son's rejection or foolishness. He did not ask where he had been or why he smelled like a pig. What did the dad do?

- He called for the "best robe."

- He put a "ring on his finger."

- He placed "sandals on his feet."

- He ordered the servants to "bring the fattened calf and kill it. Let's have a feast and celebrate. For this son of mine was dead and is alive again; he was lost and is found."

Each action has a spiritual application.

1. The robe. When you confess Christ as your Savior and ask Him to forgive your sin, you are clothed in the righteousness of Christ. Christ's righteousness is your robe. This demonstrates that God has forgiven and accepted you, and when He looks at you, He sees the righteousness of Christ, not your sin: "God made Him who had no sin to be sin for us, so that in Him we might become the righteousness of God" (2 Cor. 5:21).

2. The ring. When you trust Christ to be your Savior, you are adopted into the family of God by faith. You become an heir of God. The ring is a symbol of restored relationship. The son received his father's signet ring, which indicated he was once again part of the family: "For you did not receive a Spirit that makes you a slave again to fear, but you received the Spirit of sonship. And by Him we cry, 'Abba, Father.' The Spirit Himself testifies with our spirit that we are God's children. Now if we are

children, then we are heirs—heirs of God and co-heirs with
Christ" (Rom. 8:15–17).

3. *The sandals.* The sandals were to bring comfort and protection to the son's bruised and aching feet. When you confess
Christ as your Savior, you become the dwelling place of God
(Eph. 2:22). The Holy Spirit dwells in you to be your comfort
and strength. Jesus said, "I will ask the Father, and He will give
you another Counselor to be with you forever—the Spirit of
truth. The world cannot accept Him, because it neither sees Him
nor knows Him. But you know Him, for He lives with you and
will be in you" (John 14:16–17). After Jesus returned to heaven
following His resurrection, the Holy Spirit was sent to be our
Counselor—providing comfort and strength.

4. *The celebration.* Jesus said, "I tell you that . . . there will be
more rejoicing in heaven over one sinner who repents than over
ninety-nine righteous persons who do not need to repent" (Luke
15:7). The desire of God's heart is that the men and women He
created live in relationship with Him. When you respond to
Him, He accepts you as His child, and then it's party time in
heaven! Has heaven celebrated over you?

Have you experienced God's forgiveness? Or are you like
many people in our world who choose to live their own way, with
guilt and bitterness? If you want to experience true joy and freedom in this life, you must experience God's forgiveness. You also
must practice forgiveness as a way of life.

The Father Replaced Symbols of Separation

Third, the father replaced every symbol of separation at the
time of the reunion. The father covered his son's poverty with
his robe of luxury: "Bring the best robe and put it on him." His
status changed again: "Put a ring on his finger." He was once a

servant to the owner of the pigpen, but the ring of ownership/authority was back on his finger. The son's want was replaced with the father's plenty: "Bring the fattened calf and kill it. Let's have a feast and celebrate." Once he hungered, eating the husks of the corn left by the pigs. Now he feasted on the "fattened calf," the one his father had been preparing for the occasion.

If people only knew the welcome the heavenly Father is preparing, they wouldn't delay their journey to Him! Every "worst" is replaced with God's "best." Every lack is replaced with His supply. Sorrow is turned to celebration.

The Father Decreed a New Condition

Fourth, the father decreed a new condition: "This son of mine was dead and is alive; he was lost and is found." The found son experienced a change of status in his community, and he experienced a new condition in his heart. His father decreed that his "death" was considered "life." His "lostness" was declared "found." The father never stopped loving him, but the son made decisions that changed his condition. The reunion saw a change in his condition.

It's the same in our spiritual restoration with God. He decrees a change in our spiritual condition. The Bible says, "Because of His great love for us, God, who is rich in mercy, made us alive with Christ even when we were dead in transgressions" (Eph. 2:4–5).

This story of the lost son offers my favorite description of God. He longs for you to come to Him. When you make the decision to respond to His love, He will run to meet you! He is waiting for you. I pray you will not wait another moment to experience His forgiveness. *Please come home!*

THE DWELLING PLACE OF GOD

One of the most beautiful homes I have ever visited was on the fourth story of an old apartment building in downtown Timisoara, Romania. That evening, I had the pleasure of speaking at my good friend Peter Dugulescu's church, First Baptist of Timisoara. Following the service, we drove across the city to have dinner with a church member. The dear family invited us warmly into their home, saying the Romanian Christian greeting, "Pache" (peace).

I have learned to expect the conditions most Romanians live in, but I was still surprised to find a family of five living in an apartment with only three tiny rooms. Twenty of us crowded around makeshift tables stretched through the main room. Somehow, in a kitchen smaller than many American bathrooms, our hostess had made a four-star meal. Most memorable of all was the sweet spirit of the parents and children. They respected and served each other and us graciously. Their faces glowed with Christian love. I was blessed by spending a few hours in their home, and I was reminded that a home has no relation to a house. A home is intangible—it consists of loving acceptance and family relationships. I cannot help wondering how many broken hearts would exchange a house filled with everything money can buy for a home, if they only knew the difference.

Paul was an enemy of the early church who cruelly opposed and persecuted many Christians. While traveling to the city of Damascus, Paul had a dramatic encounter with Christ. His life was transformed through faith in the Lord Jesus Christ, and he became one of the great leaders of the church.

As a believer, Paul was personally subjected to religious persecution, and he was banished to a Roman prison for proclaiming his faith. From that dungeon, he wrote a letter of instruction and encouragement to the Christians ("Christ-ones") living around the major metropolitan city, Ephesus.

This letter, circulated among the Ephesian Christians, is one of the stellar books of the Bible. It teaches us about the Lord Jesus Christ's relationship with His people, their relationship with each other, and their place in this world—and the world to come.

THE DWELLING PLACE

When we commit our lives to Christ, He comes to dwell in us by His Spirit. Paul declared,

> Through Him we both have access to the Father by one Spirit. Consequently, you are no longer foreigners and aliens, but fellow citizens with God's people and members of God's household, built on the foundation of the apostles and prophets, with Christ Jesus Himself as the Chief Cornerstone. In Him the whole building is joined together and rises to become a holy temple in the Lord. *And in Him you too are being built together to become a dwelling in which God lives by His Spirit.* (Eph. 2:18–22, emphasis mine)

This passage is one of my favorites in the Bible. Whenever I feel overwhelmed or discouraged, I rely on these verses. I try to grasp the realization that the God of all creation is living in me. I am the dwelling place of God.

It's such an important truth. Not only do you and I belong to God through faith in His Son, the Lord Jesus Christ; He also belongs to us. He came to *dwell among us* in the person of His Son to provide for our salvation. And He came to *dwell in us* in the person of His Holy Spirit to give us an assurance of our relationship with Him and to empower us to become more like Him.

You are a spiritual building inhabited by the God of the universe. God—who knew you even before He laid the foundations of this world—now *lives in* you through your faith in His Son.

What a great progression! First, you become aware that He is looking for you, longing for you to live in relationship with Him. Then, you apply His provision of forgiveness and acceptance to your life by trusting the promises of His Word. Finally you understand that He has taken up residence in your life. Your heart is His home.

YOUR HEART, GOD'S HOME

Have you ever invited a cleaning service to restore order to your house? Maybe it's your annual spring-cleaning or an after-moving scrub-down. In any case, you can't eliminate the filth by yourself. But when the professional cleaners arrive, do you forbid them to enter the dirtiest rooms? Of course, that sounds ridiculous. The garage or bathrooms are the main reasons you hired professional cleaners. Yet many Christians invite God into their lives to bring cleansing and renewal, but try to exclude Him from certain dirty rooms.

When you make a commitment to follow the Lord Jesus Christ, you give Him ownership of your heart. Christ comes to "dwell in your [heart] through faith" (Eph. 3:17). As a result, according to God's Word, your heart becomes the dwelling place of God: "As God has said: 'I will live with them and walk among them, and I will be their God, and they will be My people'" (2 Cor. 6:16). Your heart is a place where God lives. As He lives in you, "His power . . . is at work" within you (Eph. 3:20). He is there "24/7"—every hour of every day. His Holy Spirit walks throughout your "house," speaking words of friendship, acceptance, and love. He has taken responsibility over every area of your life. You can't compartmentalize your heart or reject the Spirit's intervention in especially "dirty" areas.

Let's study the spiritual implications of God's inhabiting your heart as His dwelling place.

WHY IS HE THERE?

Can you imagine a Wall Street executive decorating his office with the same posters and lava lamps his son at college uses to decorate a dorm room? Every office complex, dorm room, and house reflects the inhabitant's personality, vision, and skills. The dwelling place of your heart is a reflection of God's glory and creative purpose. Paul told believers, "We are God's fellow workers; you are God's field, *God's building*" (1 Cor. 3:9, emphasis mine).

You are a living testimonial of God's forgiveness, restoration, and acceptance. When the world sees your spiritual "building," the world is directed to the Master Builder who envisioned it, framed it, and spiritually renovated it. That's why it is important for you to maintain the property spiritually. You are an example to others of the purpose and skills of the One who created you. The Spirit enables you to bear the fruit of a growing life in Christ, exemplifying "goodness, righteousness and truth" (Eph. 5:9). "So whether you eat or drink or whatever you do, do it all for the glory of God" (1 Cor. 10:31).

Ephesians 4:3 speaks of "the unity of the Spirit." Living within each Christian, the Holy Spirit brings unity, making us the body of Christ.

God's ultimate reason for establishing a relationship with you through the forgiveness of your sins and filling your heart with His Spirit is simple. Jesus said, "I have come that they may have life, and have it to the full" (John 10:10).

A UNIQUE DWELLING

My good friend Mark Yoder worked for years as one of our community's best general contractors. He developed two large subdivisions—Willow West and Windsor Estates. The Yoder & Sons crew built the houses in those developments. There are similarities in the way each house was built—the types of basic lumber and cinder block and the crew's signature touches of quality and style. Yet no two houses are the same. The builder's imprint is clear, but the details always differ. House designs, colors, and fixtures are unique—like our spiritual buildings.

Physically all of us are "special orders." God created us individually and uniquely. We may share characteristics with the human race, but we are distinctly original. Our uniqueness extends all the way to the tips of our fingers. Each of us has a unique set of fingerprints. With DNA testing, a piece of my hair or a drop of my blood can prove my identity. There are no duplicates among six billion of us. Now that's unique!

Some people want us to believe that this grand design accidentally happened. But you are no accident. God designed and created you. Inspired by the Holy Spirit, the psalmist David wrote,

> For You created my inmost being;
>> You knit me together in my mother's womb.
> I praise You because I am fearfully and wonderfully made;
>> Your works are wonderful,
>> I know that full well. (Ps. 139:13–14)

As a boy, I watched Ethel Waters sing at the Billy Graham crusades. She often sang "His Eye Is on the Sparrow." She would begin by sharing a brief testimony. Then just before the song, she would say, "Honey, God made you, and He doesn't make any junk!"

Psychologically we may share characteristics with others. Maybe you've taken a personality test that nailed you as "sanguine" or "melancholy." Yet we all cry and laugh, experience fear and excitement. We share many similar motivations and desires. But each of us has a personality unlike any other.

Even our individual genealogies make us different. We come from particular environments that have molded our actions and reactions. We have different strengths and weaknesses. You and I are unique persons. As the classic jingle in an insurance advertisement said, "There's nobody else in the whole human race with your kind of style and your kind of grace."

We are also unique spiritually. We have a relationship with God that is unlike any other person's. Your relationship with God is tailor-made. It fits your physiological and psychological characteristics. You and I are unique dwelling places of God.

A DWELLING UNDER CONSTRUCTION

In his letter to the Ephesians, Paul said that the dwelling is, "built on the foundation of the apostles and prophets, with Christ Jesus Himself as the chief cornerstone. In Him the whole building is joined together and rises to become a holy temple in the Lord. And in Him you too are being built together to become a dwelling in which God lives by His Spirit" (Eph. 2:20–22). Notice that the dwelling is a work in progress—"you . . . are being built."

If you've ever moved into a brand-new home, you know what it is like to live in a dwelling under construction. The move is just the beginning. There seems to be an endless number of projects necessary for the completion of your new dwelling: painting the trim, installing lighting and carpeting, adding appliances, and, overall, customizing to fit your personal tastes.

Likewise, as a dwelling place of God, you are under construction. In a letter to Christians in Philippi, Paul wrote, "He who began a good work in you will carry it on to completion until the day of Christ Jesus" (Phil. 1:6). In other words, as long as you're on the earth, you are a spiritual project under construction.

Following the Lord Jesus Christ is not a one-time experience; it's a way of life. Becoming like Him in your thoughts, your words, and your actions takes daily spiritual development. Just as an earthly building is built brick by brick, floor by floor, and room by room, so your spiritual dwelling is completed in stages.

The first stage in your spiritual development—your foundation—is your confession of your need for Christ. This is when you are converted—the most important decision in your life. This is the moment that your heart becomes Christ's home and Christ becomes your foundation. God has a master plan that is perfect for you.

Other stages of development follow. You learn to love God's Word as you develop a routine for daily Scripture reading. You learn the benefits of a daily conversation with God (prayer). You learn how to tell others about God. Even your Scripture reading and prayer grow more meaningful over time. With proper attention, every area of your Christian life will improve, the longer you walk with Christ. I used to wear a pin on my baseball jacket: "PBPGINFWMY." It was a great opportunity to witness and an encouraging reminder for myself: "Please Be Patient. God Is Not Finished With Me Yet."

The beautiful part about this newfound relationship is that you can trust God to do what is best. He wants you to achieve your maximum potential. He resides in you to help you become all He created you to be. God is on your side. The foundation has been laid, but that is just the beginning. He wants to build on that foundation. Read Ephesians 2:10: "For we are God's workmanship, created in Christ Jesus to do good works, which God prepared in advance for us to do." That is an awesome statement. Did you realize that God has things that He has prepared for you to do? To fulfill God's plans for you, you must build properly so you can become the person God wants you to be.

I remember the day Barbara and I brought Michelle, our firstborn child, home from the hospital. I was definitely a happy, excited, and proud dad. We had decorated and prepared Michelle's room in anticipation of her birth. God had blessed us with a beautiful baby girl, and we could not have been more thankful. What would have happened to Michelle if we had placed her on the front porch of our home and said, "You can grow up now"? Of course, that is a foolish question—she would not have survived.

I can report that we did not leave Michelle on the front porch. She is now twenty-three years old, has graduated from college, and is working as a research writer. It has been a joy for Barbara and me to see our children grow and develop into the people they are today. Just as He does with all of His children, including me, God is still shaping them according to His design. Becoming buildings that honor our Lord is a lifelong process.

A popular children's song, "He's Still Working on Me," communicates the truth of your uniqueness as well as the building process at work in your life:

> He's still working on me, making me what I ought to be,
> It took Him just a week to make the moon and stars
> The sun and earth and Jupiter and Mars
> How loving and patient He must be!
> He's still working on me.

When you say yes to Christ, you have a firm foundation. Paul warned us about building on this foundation,

> By the grace God has given me, I laid a foundation as an expert builder, and someone else is building on it. But each one should be careful how he builds. For no one can lay any foundation other than the one already laid, which is Jesus Christ. If any man builds on this foundation using gold, silver, costly stones, wood, hay or straw, his work will be shown for what it is, because the Day will bring it to light. It will be revealed with fire, and the fire will test the quality of each man's work. If what he has built survives, he will receive his reward. If it is burned up, he will suffer loss; he himself will be saved, but only as one escaping through the flames. Don't you know that you yourselves are God's temple and that God's Spirit lives in you? (1 Cor. 3:10–16)

Several basic principles will help you build on your foundation.

1. Read the Bible

As I described it earlier, the Bible is a love letter written to you. God speaks to you through His Word. To build a strong dwelling, you need to read the instruction book—the Bible. I encourage you to set a certain time each day for reading His Word. If you are not familiar with the Bible, begin with the fourth book in the New Testament, the gospel of John.

The Navigators, an international ministry of evangelism and discipleship, created a wonderful list of reminders of the importance of the Word of God and how we should apply it to our lives.

- Hear the Word. You need to hear the Word. And I am thankful that there are many ways to hear it. It is presented most often through a sermon or a Bible lesson. You can get the Bible on tape or CD and listen to it in your home or your car. You may also find a favorite Bible teacher on Christian radio or TV.

- Read the Word. As I have already mentioned, set aside daily time to read the Word. You will want to have a personal time of Bible reading. But it is also encouraging and bonding to read the Bible together as a family or a couple at breakfast or in the evening.

- Study the Word. Many excellent Bible study materials are available through your church or local Christian bookstore. Become a student of the Word of God. We are told in 2 Timothy 2:15, "Do your best to present yourself to God as one approved, a workman who does not need to be ashamed and who correctly handles the word of truth."

- Memorize the Word. "Your Word I have hidden in my heart, that I might not sin against You," wrote the psalmist in Psalm 119:11 (NKJV). The verses you have stored in your memory are an immediate defense against Satan's temptations. Memorize verses that address particular struggles you are having. When the enemy of your soul attacks, you will have an immediate guard as the Holy Spirit reminds you of the scriptures you have memorized.

- Meditate. For the Christian, meditation is simply focusing on the meaning of God's word and its application on our lives. Taking time to get rid of distractions and reflect on a section of scripture is especially important in our cluttered, modern lifestyles. Psalm 1:2–3 indicates the importance of meditation: "But his delight is in the law of the Lord, / and on His law he meditates day and night. / He is like a tree planted by streams of water, / which yields its fruit in season / and whose leaf does not wither." Meditate on key verses you have memorized. As you think quietly about the Word, the Holy Spirit speaks into your life and you grow spiritually, becoming established in your faith.

2. Pray

Throughout the New Testament, Jesus encouraged us to ask, seek, and knock. We are told in Hebrews 4:16, "Let us then approach the throne of grace with confidence, so that we may receive mercy and find grace to help us in our time of need."

In a growing relationship, communication is essential. J. Oswald Sanders wrote,

> "The Spirit links Himself with us in our prayers and pours His supplications into our own. We may master the technique of prayer and understand its philosophy; we may have unlimited confidence in the veracity and validity of the promises concerning prayer. We may plead them earnestly. But if we ignore the part played by the Holy Spirit, we have failed to use the master key."

3. Have Fellowship with Other Christians

In his book *Basic Christianity*, Dr. John R. W. Stott spoke of the body of Christ:

> "The Church . . . is the body of Christ. Every Christian is a member or organ of the body, while Christ Himself is the Head, controlling the body's activities. Not every organ has the same function, but each is necessary for the maximum health and usefulness of the body. Moreover, the whole body is animated by a common life. This is the Holy Spirit. It is His presence which makes the body one."

You must have fellowship with others who are part of the body of Christ. This fellowship should take place as a way of life. You may have an accountability partner, a Christian with whom you can share confidentially and who will keep you accountable. You may choose to pray and study the Bible together and spend time building your relationship. I also encourage you to participate in a small group of others who earnestly desire to grow in their walk with the Lord. We read in the book of Hebrews: "Let us not give up meeting together, as some are in the habit of doing, but let us encourage one another—and all the more as you see the Day approaching" (10:25).

Being associated with a church is vital to your spiritual growth. In his book *Steps to Peace with God*, Dr. Billy Graham offers helpful advice: "Each Christian should select his church because he is convinced that within its particular structure he will find the greatest opportunity for spiritual growth, the greatest satisfaction for his human needs, and the greatest chance to be of helpful service to those around him."

If you set a large pile of wood on fire, it will produce intense heat and light. If you take one of the blazing logs out of the fire, it will soon be extinguished. United with the body of Christ, your little log is part of a roaring bonfire. By joining with other Christians, you receive encouragement and strength to grow in your relationship with the Lord. You need to be actively involved in a local church.

4. Tell Others What Christ Has Done for You

You are to be a witness for Christ. When you tell others what Christ has done in your life, you grow spiritually. The Bible explains,

> They overcame him [the devil]
>> by the blood of the Lamb
>> and by the word of their testimony. (Rev. 12:11)

When you share your faith with someone, keep several things in mind:

- Make your story personal—you want to tell the person what Christ has done in your life.

- Keep your story short and interesting—three minutes is a good goal.

- Place Christ at the center of your story.

- Always use a verse or two of Scripture. The Word of God has power.

The following principles have been vitally important in my spiritual growth. I pray that they will be a great help to you.

MAINTAINING THE DWELLING

The apostle Paul gave instructions for maintaining your spiritual dwelling. To a new Christian named Timothy, he wrote, "Guard the good deposit that was entrusted to you—guard it with the help of the Holy Spirit who lives in us" (2 Tim. 1:14). God's benefits are given to you as a living trust. You are a spiritual trustee of His riches ("the good deposit"; see also 1 Cor. 4:1–2). In the material realm, the duties of a trustee include the upkeep and security of the building.

You have maintenance duties for your spiritual dwelling. But you have help—"the help of the Holy Spirit who lives in us." God not only lives in you; He also acts as your new landlord. He has provided all the tools and resources you need to fulfill your responsibilities, but you have to use them. Let's look at your responsibilities in light of God's help.

1. You Have the Responsibility of Security

Paul advised Timothy to be on guard. He also told the Corinthians, "Be on your guard; stand firm in the faith" (1 Cor. 16:13). Just as a trustee works to ensure that earthly property is kept safe from intruders, so you have a responsibility to guard your spiritual dwelling from intruders.

The enemy of your faith, Satan, seeks to destroy your spiritual dwelling. The Bible cautions, "Be self-controlled and alert. Your enemy the devil prowls around like a roaring lion looking for someone to devour" (1 Peter 5:8). You must make every effort to be sure that he doesn't cross your spiritual property lines. You do that by rejecting the entertainment, affiliations, and affections that he delights in.

Remember, the Holy Spirit lives within you to help you. He is faithful to provide an inner warning (much like a motion-detector security light) when the enemy is intruding. You learn to listen to the Holy Spirit's inner voice—usually speaking through your conscience—when you make choices.

2. You Must Keep Up Your Spiritual Dwelling

Just as basic maintenance—for example, cleaning and painting—improves the appearance of your earthly dwelling, so a little maintenance will improve the appearance of your spiritual dwelling. I'm not referring to plastic surgery, makeup, or a bodybuilding program. I'm referring to a changed life. As you allow Christ to be who He already is in you, His presence will be evidenced in you. How will it be evidenced? It will be evidenced in your walk (the way you live your life). It will be evidenced in the way you talk (your conversation will be controlled by Him). It will be evidenced in the way you think (you have the "mind of Christ").

Your spiritual dwelling must be a *positive* dwelling. A follower of Christ reflects the hope that He brings to your heart: "Christ in you, the hope of glory" (Col. 1:27). In the face of alarming news headlines and doomsday predictions, the child of God exudes a spirit of confidence. The apostle Peter instructed his Christian brothers and sisters, "Always be prepared to give an answer to everyone who asks you to give the reason for the hope that you have. But do this with gentleness and respect" (1 Peter 3:15).

Your spiritual dwelling must be a *pure* dwelling. Your automobile is subject to the dirt and grime of the road. "Wash Me!" someone writes in the dust on a rear window. And you finally go to the car wash, especially before a special occasion or trip to the in-laws. After all, you understand that appearance reflects the values and habits of the owner.

It's the same with your spiritual dwelling. You want to be free from the dirt and grime of our sinful society. You want your values, actions, and affections to truly reflect those of your Owner and Inhabiter, the Lord Jesus Christ.

Your spiritual dwelling is a *progressive* dwelling. Certain architecture is said to be dated or identified with an architectural period such as Victorian or contemporary. Your spiritual dwelling, however, reflects both the old and the new. It's built by ancient standards—the eternal principles of God's Word. And it's new because it reflects the ever-new mercies of its true Owner: "His compassions never fail. They are new every morning" (Lam. 3:22–23). Even as Victorian homes have contemporary furnishings and fixtures, your spiritual dwelling has a contemporary flair. You apply ancient truths in a modern setting—without compromising those truths.

3. You Have Confirmation of Ownership

Usually a building's owner locks the deed and official documents in a bank vault. An owner knows that a written right of ownership is clear proof of ownership.

The "rights" to your spiritual dwelling are even more secure.

A God who cannot lie confirmed them. The writer to the Hebrew Christians declared:

> Men swear by someone greater than themselves, and the oath confirms what is said and puts an end to all argument. Because God wanted to make the unchanging nature of His purpose very clear to the heirs of what was promised, He confirmed it with an oath. God did this so that, by two unchangeable things in which it is impossible for God to lie, we who have fled to take hold of the hope offered to us may be greatly encouraged. We have this hope as an anchor for the soul, firm and secure. (Heb. 6:16–19)

God's Word, the Bible, thoroughly documents your rights. John, a disciple of Jesus, wrote that the Bible's words "are written that you may believe that Jesus is the Christ, the Son of God, and that by believing you may have life in His name" (John 20:31). The Bible is not only the best-selling book of all time; it has been tested and proved true in the lives of those who have lived by its principles.

An inner witness verifies your rights. You've probably taken a business trip or a vacation when you wished you could be home. And you know the feeling of returning after a long absence and walking through the front door with the unmistakable relief that you are finally home—you know that this is where you belong.

God verifies in your heart that you are a spiritual dwelling. You have the inner sense that He belongs there and you are at home in His presence. Paul wrote, "You did not receive a spirit that makes you a slave again to fear, but you received the Spirit of sonship . . . The Spirit himself testifies with our spirit that we are God's children" (Rom. 8:15–16).

You have the witness of others. A witness can be called to testify about the authenticity of property rights. The witness verifies the ownership of a property in question. When it comes to the authenticity of your spiritual dwelling, there are witnesses to provide verification.

By the changes in your attitude and actions, loved ones and friends will verify that you are a spiritual dwelling. Jesus spoke about being spiritually authentic: "By their fruit you will recognize them. Do people pick grapes from thornbushes, or figs from thistles? Likewise every good tree bears good fruit, but a bad tree bears bad fruit" (Matt. 7:16–17). Those who are inhabited by God have godly qualities.

Isn't it wonderful to know that God offers you loving acceptance, forgiveness, and spiritual help? And isn't it wonderful to know that through personal faith in the Lord Jesus Christ, He has brought all of that to His dwelling—your heart?

6

ASSURANCE

No matter where you are in your spiritual journey, there will be times when you experience spiritual doubt. During Christ's ministry on earth, even His closest disciples lacked inner assurance at times. But it is important for all of God's children to be assured of our relationship with God. You can, and should, be certain that God has forgiven you of your sin and accepted you into His family. God wants you to know without a doubt that you now belong to Him. In the Bible He tells new believers: "Do you not know that your body is a temple of the Holy Spirit, who is in you, whom you have received from God? You are not your own; you were bought at a price" (1 Cor. 6:19–20).

Following the awful and awesome events of Christ's crucifixion and His miraculous resurrection from the grave, Jesus' disciples were in a state of spiritual and emotional limbo. They faced persecution from those who had executed their Leader. They had personally witnessed the miracle of His resurrection when Jesus appeared after His death at one of their gatherings. Yet they faced an uncertain future. They knew that Jesus had promised them a lasting and important ministry. But the turmoil of recent events raised some major questions: What would they do with their lives? What would be their future? The disciples were filled with fear and confusion when Jesus appeared to them once again:

> Afterward Jesus appeared again to His disciples, by the Sea of Tiberias. It happened this way: Simon Peter, Thomas (called Didymus), Nathanael from Cana in Galilee, the sons of Zebedee, and two other disciples were together. "I'm going out to fish," Simon Peter told them, and they said, "We'll go with you." So they went out and got into the boat, but that night they caught nothing. Early in the morning, Jesus stood on the shore, but the disciples did not realize that it was Jesus. He called out to them, "Friends, haven't you any fish?" "No," they answered. He said, "Throw your net on the right side of the boat and you will find some." When they did, they were unable to haul the net in because of the large number of fish. Then the disciple whom Jesus loved said to Peter. "It is the Lord!" As soon as Simon Peter heard him say, "It is the Lord," he wrapped his outer garment around him (for he had taken it off) and jumped into the water. The other disciples followed in the boat, towing the net full of fish, for they were not far from shore, about a hundred yards. (John 21:1–8)

IMPORTANT TRUTHS

One of the disciples, Peter, made a decision, and the rest followed: "I'm going out to fish." It was more than a recreational decision. It was vocational and spiritual. Before they followed Jesus and were part of His earthly ministry, most of the disciples were fishermen by trade. Now that Jesus was gone, Peter and the others returned to fishing. Essentially they were saying, "We don't know what's going to happen next, or if the amazing events of the last few years are over. So let's just go back to what we know and where we were before we met Jesus." Doubts had crept into their hearts.

The dialogue between Jesus on the shore and the disciples returning from a whole night of unsuccessful fishing is very revealing. It demonstrates six important truths.

1. Jesus Cared Deeply About Those Who Followed Him

He met them at their point of need. When the disciples were in confusion, He immediately made His way to their side. You can always be assured that Christ will be at your side during crises—spiritual or otherwise. He promised,

> "Never will I leave you;
> never will I forsake you."
> So we say with confidence,
> "The Lord is my helper; I will not be afraid.
> What can man do to me?" (Heb. 13:5–6)

2. Listeners Did Not Immediately Understand His Words

Instead of encouraging the exhausted fishermen, Jesus asked them a direct and disturbing question: "Friends, haven't you any fish?" He wanted them to think about their present condition in light of His previous promises. When He first called the disciples to follow Him, Jesus gave them a purpose and a promise: "'Come, follow me,' Jesus said, 'and I will make you fishers of men'" (Matt. 4:19). When you have spiritual doubts, begin by facing them directly. You must acknowledge your questions before you can deal with them. Then examine each doubt in light of God's promises that He has given to you in His Word.

We may not easily understand God's workings in our lives, but they will always be true to His Word. He tells us,

"My thoughts are not your thoughts,
neither are your ways My ways,"
    declares the LORD.
"As the heavens are higher than the earth,
so are My ways higher than your ways
and My thoughts than your thoughts." (Isa. 55:8–9)

He has the Master Plan. His salvation is dependable even when we can't fully understand it. He never breaks a promise.

Several weeks after I asked Christ to forgive my sins and come into my life, I began to feel guilty for my sin. I was beginning to doubt my salvation. One morning, I had been reading my Bible and praying about all the things I had done wrong. I discovered later what was happening: Satan was attacking my mind. He was causing me to doubt my salvation. He encouraged me to dwell on memories of my life without Christ. That morning I was kneeling beside my bed and confessing again all the sins I could remember. While I was digging up my past sins, God spoke to my heart. I heard His words as clearly as if He had spoken audibly. He said, *What are you talking about?*

God reminded me of two verses I had memorized:

As far as the east is from the west,
    so far has He removed our transgressions from us. (Ps. 103:12)

For I will forgive their wickedness
    and will remember their sins no more. (Jer. 31:34)

I was reminded through His Word that He had forgiven me, and He had forgotten all about my past. I was a completely new creation: "Therefore, if anyone is in Christ, he is a new creation; the old has gone, the new has come!" (2 Cor. 5:17). I was filled with joy and freedom. I came to the realization that I am forgiven and accepted.

3. Jesus Challenged the Disciples to Trust Him Despite Their Doubts

"Throw your net on the right side of the boat and you will find some," He said. Like a loving earthly father encouraging his child to jump down into his arms, Jesus invited His followers to take a leap of faith into His security. He wanted them to trust Him in spite of their confusion, questions, and despair.

You, too, may have no idea how Christ will deliver you, but you can rest on the fact that up to this point, He has kept every promise. And your faith will be assured as you continue to walk in obedience to His Word. Jesus said, "If anyone loves Me, he will keep My word; and My Father will love him, and We will come to him and make Our home with him" (John 14:23 NKJV).

A principle that has helped me throughout my walk of faith with Christ is looking at the examples of spiritual giants. My faith is stretched as I see how God has blessed and provided for men and women who walked in faith despite major obstacles. Of course, our primary example is Jesus, but it is also biblical to learn from heroes of the faith. We can receive encouragement and hope as we study the lives of God's faithful servants. One of those godly examples is Joshua, who led the Israelite nation after Moses died. By the end of Joshua's life, "not one of all the LORD's good promises to the house of Israel failed; every one was fulfilled" (Josh. 21:45). What a statement! Read and study the life of Joshua and be encouraged. He went through major trials and disappointments. Yet at the end of his life he could proclaim that "not one of all the LORD's good promises . . . failed." That's the kind of person I want to spend time with!

If you are looking for some good books to encourage you in this area, I recommend two by Dr. Warren Wiersbe, *Walking with the Giants* and *Listening to the Giants*. They are short biographies of men and women God has used in a mighty way.

4. Jesus Rewarded Their Faith with Fullness

"When they did [throw the net to the other side of the boat as Jesus directed], they were unable to haul the net in because of the large number of fish." When the disciples obeyed the Lord and rested on His promise, He miraculously affirmed their trust. The Master knew that His disciples' faith needed a trial run. Their assurance came from their experience. You will make a similar discovery. The more you trust and obey the Lord Jesus Christ, the more you will find Him to be trustworthy. You will see evidence of His faithfulness to you. One day you may begin to see your trials as opportunities to watch God work.

5. The Presence of the Lord Is Greater Than the Problem

The disciples were victorious over their doubts. At first they didn't recognize who was giving the commands. And they didn't understand what difference the commands would make in their lives. But they knew that only one Person was worthy of their unqualified trust. One of the disciples recognized the presence of the risen Christ. And then the very one who had set the corporate doubts in motion ran to Jesus: "As soon as Simon Peter heard him say, 'It is the Lord,' he wrapped his outer garment around him . . . and jumped into the water."

The unconditional love and acceptance of the Lord Jesus Christ had touched Peter's life. He loved the Master enough to trust Him in spite of his personal doubts or confusion. Later, that same disciple taught other Christians about trusting Christ. He wrote, "Though you have not seen Him [Christ], you love Him; and even though you do not see Him now, you believe in Him and are filled with an inexpressible and glorious joy" (1 Peter 1:8).

In the book of Hebrews we read, "Now faith is being sure of what we hope for and certain of *what we do not see*" (Heb. 11:1, emphasis mine). Your inner, spiritual assurance begins with trusting God to keep His promises to you. As you learn to accept His promises, you will continue to grow in your walk of faith.

6. Faith Is Contagious

"The other disciples followed in the boat, towing the net full of fish." Peter's enthusiastic response to the presence of the Lord Jesus Christ in the midst of his prevailing doubts was an encouragement to others. They followed him. Acting on the inner assurance that God brings to your heart will have a positive impact on others.

CHRIST WANTS YOU TO BE SURE

At times, believers in Christ from every walk of life struggle with the same question: "Am I really a Christian?" For some, the questioning is traumatic. They live with the fear that they are not saved. For others, the questioning is less intense. It is a quiet, persistent nagging in the back of the mind: *Can I really be sure I'm saved?*

Christ wants you to be sure of your relationship with Him. He wants you to experience a spiritually courageous and confident relationship with Him. His Word (the Bible) is filled with promises that affirm that relationship. One of the most outstanding is found in a letter written by one of Jesus' disciples, the apostle John. In the days of early Christianity, the Bible as we know it was not available. Early Christians read the Old Testament scriptures on scrolls of papyrus. As you can imagine, that took real effort, and there were few copies. Some scholars say that one book of Old Testament scriptures was more than sixty feet long!

To bring additional instruction and assurance to His people, God communicated His truth and His promises through the writings of the apostles (missionary leaders) of the early church. The apostle John wrote a letter that was circulated among the Christians who met in house churches.

It was a letter of instruction about Christian beliefs. It warned the new Christians about false teachings that were prevalent in their day (as false teachings are also prevalent today). It was also a letter of encouragement to affirm the Christian believers in their relationship with God. The first of John's three letters taught about assurance: "And this is the testimony: God has given us eternal life, and this life is in his Son. He who has the Son has life; he who does not have the Son of God does not have life. I write these things to you who believe in the name of the Son of God so that you may know that you have eternal life" (1 John 5:11–13).

FEELINGS OR FACTS?

What reassurance! Our relationship with God is not based on a "hope-so" experience. It is a "know-so" relationship. No matter how we feel about it on a particular day, we can know that we have eternal life if we believe in the name of the Son of God. Our assurance is based not on human emotions, but on the facts of God's Word.

The experience of being forgiven and accepted by God

through faith in the Lord Jesus Christ certainly involves feelings. We are emotional beings. God has enabled us to have joy and hope. We love. We feel inner peace. We cry tears of relief and repentance. There is definitely an emotional side to salvation. But emotions are as varied as the personalities and characteristics of people. Some feel exuberant joy when they give their hearts to Christ. Many feel quiet peacefulness and relief. Others feel nothing at all!

Feelings differ. But your salvation does not depend upon how you feel about it. Rather, it depends upon what God has done about it! Paul explained, "'The word is near you; it is in your mouth and in your heart,' that is, the word of faith we are proclaiming: That if you confess with your mouth, 'Jesus is Lord,' and believe in your heart that God raised him from the dead, you will be saved" (Rom. 10:8–9). Note, "You *will* be saved."

One of my favorite illustrations comes from Dr. Bill Bright, the founder of Campus Crusade for Christ. I was in Chicago at a conference on evangelism almost twenty-five years ago when Dr. Bright shared this illustration. I hope it will prove to be helpful to you.

A train will run with or without the caboose. Put fuel in the locomotive (or facts), and the train is guaranteed to run. The caboose (feeling) is a part of the train, but it does not power the train. In the same way, if you put your faith in the fact, you will be saved. Your faith, no matter how small, is the spark that is needed to ignite the power of God. Feelings are part of who we are, but they do not dictate our relationship with Christ. Feelings are fickle. Some days I feel good, some days I feel bad, and other days I'm in neutral.

People have asked me, "What does a Christian feel like?"

That question cannot be answered. I am a Christian, and I have many different feelings. If you had called me last winter when I had the flu, I would have said this Christian had a headache and a churning stomach and was breaking out in cold sweats. In short, I felt lousy. If you talked to me the day my son, David, left for a six-month mission term in Bolivia, I would have said I felt an intense mixture of joy, thankfulness, sadness, and pride. As individuals, we have different types of emotions and feelings that can change from moment to moment. Our feelings depend upon our circumstances. But our relationship with Christ is constant. My salvation is based on faith in the fact. Feelings follow along on the ride of life. They never determine its outcome. My faith in Christ determines the outcome.

You may say, "But I'm not good enough for God," and I would agree. You're 100 percent right. We can't ever do anything to be good enough for God. All of us have sinned against Him. (See Rom. 3:23.) His acceptance and forgiveness are gifts given to us through the sacrifice of His only Son, the Lord Jesus Christ. Your relationship with Him is based not on how good you are but on how good He is! "It is because of Him that you are in Christ Jesus, who has become for us wisdom from God—that is, our righteousness, holiness and redemption" (1 Cor. 1:30).

THE ASSURANCE OF GOD'S FORGIVENESS

You decided to give your heart to Christ because you saw the spiritual need in your life. You sensed a spiritual vacuum in the depths of your being. Something was clearly missing, and your life was anything but perfect. You came to Christ because you saw that He graciously wanted to forgive you and free you from your past of sin. You trusted His Word. And God has kept His word to you! "If we confess our sins, He is faithful and just to forgive us our sins and to cleanse us from all unrighteousness" (1 John 1:9 NKJV).

The Old Testament writer exulted, "When we were overwhelmed by sins, you forgave our transgressions" (Ps. 65:3). In other words, "Lord, when we couldn't do anything to achieve forgiveness, You accomplished it for us!" You and I took the step of asking God to forgive our past sins, and He did!

> I acknowledged my sin to You,
> And my iniquity I have not hidden.
> I said, "I will confess my transgressions to the LORD,"
> And You forgave the iniquity of my sin. (Ps. 32:5 NKJV)

But you have a spiritual enemy: "Be self-controlled and alert. Your enemy the devil prowls around like a roaring lion looking for someone to devour" (1 Peter 5:8). He would like nothing better than to convince you that you are still captive to your old sinning self. He brings haunting memories of past decisions to your mind. Satan plants doubt in your mind, asking, "Could God actually forgive you?" He overwhelms you with a sense of your wrongdoing and tries to make you forget the grace of God you discovered when you gave your heart to Christ.

God's promise of forgiveness is clear: "If You, LORD, should mark iniquities, O Lord, who could stand? But there is forgiveness with You" (Ps. 130:3–4 NKJV). You were once separated from God; you are now separated from your sins. God is all-knowing and all-powerful. He could remember every sin you ever thought about committing if He chose to. Yet God mercifully chooses to forget your sins when you ask Him for forgiveness.

That's what forgiveness is. Because of His love for you, and because He longs for a relationship with you, God chooses to forget the wrongs of your past. He allows you to start a new life in Him with no condemning past: "Therefore, there is now no condemnation for those who are in Christ Jesus" (Rom. 8:1).

THE ASSURANCE OF GOD'S LOVE

God, in His very essence, is love. Nothing can separate you from His love—not even sin. The apostle Paul wrote, "For I am convinced that neither death nor life, neither angels nor demons, neither the present nor the future, nor any powers, neither height nor depth, nor anything else in all creation, will be able to separate us from the love of God that is in Christ Jesus our Lord" (Rom. 8:38–39).

God still loves you even if He hates the sin in your life. He does not excuse sin. His holiness cannot tolerate it, and He is very clear that sin has consequences. But just as earthly parents do not stop loving their children when they disobey, God loves you in spite of your actions. He longs for you to be in a pure relationship with Him; His love endures forever.

God's love is not just an intangible, feel-good characteristic. He vividly demonstrates His love. As we have seen, He showed us His love by sacrificing His only Son to pay the penalty for our disobedience. Paul explained, "God demonstrates His own love for us in this: While we were still sinners, Christ died for us" (Rom. 5:8). God gave us the gift of Himself to demonstrate how much He truly values us.

God also expresses His reassuring love to us each day. He gives us gifts of peace and inner joy. He confirms a sense of security in Him through prayer. He offers hope for the future because we know that He will be faithful to lead us. God cannot be anything but love. It would be against His nature. He confirms this in Isaiah 54:10:

> "Though the mountains be shaken
>> and the hills be removed,
> yet My unfailing love for you will not be shaken
>> nor My covenant of peace be removed,"
> says the LORD, who has compassion on you.

THE ASSURANCE OF GOD'S ACCEPTANCE

As we have already seen, when God forgave you of your past rebellion against His Word and His will, He forgave you unconditionally, and He established a loving and accepting relationship with you. God accepts you unconditionally.

That is a strange concept in a society that seeks acceptance in many material ways. From the way you dress, to your corporate image, to the automobile you drive, modern society says, "You'll be accepted *if*. . ." God accepts you, *period*! Through faith in the Lord Jesus Christ, you are immediately considered "good enough" for God. (See 1 Cor. 1:30.) The Bible describes this experience through the words of the prophet:

> The LORD your God is with you,
>> He is mighty to save.
> He will take great delight in you,
>> He will quiet you with His love,
>> He will rejoice over you with singing. (Zeph. 3:17)

God enjoys the company of His children. That is an awesome thought. God delights in you! The entire purpose of salvation is to bring you into harmony with Him.

THE ASSURANCE OF GOD'S STRENGTH

Lack of spiritual assurance comes when people can't seem to comprehend that their sins can really be forgotten. They may say, "I know that I asked for forgiveness, but I still feel guilty." Remember that feelings are fickle and changing. We cannot rely on our feelings. The Bible is very clear on this subject; God is "mighty to save." Your salvation is based on what God has done. And the apostle Paul added, "Finally, be strong in the Lord and in His mighty power" (Eph. 6:10).

The psalmist wrote about God's strength in a psalm of praise:

> One thing God has spoken,
> > two things have I heard:
> that You, O God, are strong,
> > and that You, O Lord, are loving. (Ps. 62:11–12)

God does not use power and strength to abuse, as the world often does. Instead, He combines His strength and love to graciously rescue us from the evil one. God is able to do all that He has promised. He is committed to bringing people to salvation and joy. God, the Creator of the universe, is certainly powerful enough to forgive and forget—powerful enough to rescue you from your past and give you a glorious future.

I want to paint a word picture for you that I pray will help you with the assurance of your salvation. As you know, all of us are guilty before God because all of us have sinned. Yes, some people have been far worse than others, but all sin separates us from a holy God. Not only is God holy; He is also all-knowing. Did you realize there is a set of books in heaven where God has recorded everything you and I have ever done wrong? Every word, every thought, and every wrong act is recorded in the books.

Read this passage from the very last book of the Bible:

> Then I saw a great white throne and Him who was seated on it. Earth and sky fled from His presence, and there was no place for them. And I saw the dead, great and small, standing before the throne, and books were opened. Another book was opened, which is the book of life. The dead were judged according to what they had done as recorded in the books. The sea gave up the dead that were in it, and death and Hades gave up the dead that were in them, and each person was judged according to what he had done. Then death and Hades were thrown into the lake of fire. The lake of fire is the second death. If anyone's name was not found written in the book of life, he was thrown into the lake of fire. (Rev. 20:11–15)

Here is the word picture: when you asked Christ to forgive your sin and come and live in your heart by the power of the Holy Spirit, Jesus walked to the books where all your sin was recorded. Every unkind word you ever spoke, every evil thought you ever had, and every sinful deed you ever did was recorded. All of it was there; you were guilty as charged. Jesus went to the books, and He wiped it all away.

But wait, He was not finished. He turned to the Book of Life, and with His own blood He wrote your name. Because of His grace, this work displayed through your faith in Christ alone, your name has been recorded. The devil and all of his demons cannot take that away from you. On the great day when you stand before the living God, He will look, and your name will be there.

How do you know this is true? Another attribute of God is truth. He is truth; He cannot lie. If God says it, the matter is settled.

THE ASSURANCE OF GOD'S PRESENCE

If you depend upon feelings instead of the facts of God's Word to identify whether you are a Christian, you may doubt God's presence in your life. At the moment of conversion, you may not have had a strong sense of God's presence. But God says, "I will never leave you nor forsake you" (Josh. 1:5). God is always with you. You have His Spirit dwelling inside.

Paul compared the presence of the Holy Spirit to a bank deposit. He wrote in Ephesians 1:13, "Having believed, you were marked in [God] with a seal, the promised Holy Spirit, who is a deposit guaranteeing our inheritance." The Holy Spirit is a promise of the eternal inheritance to come, and He is down payment on that inheritance. The Bible tells us He is there to assure, strengthen, enlighten, and warn us in our Christian faith (John 16).

God gives us the assurance of His presence in the good times, and He is there during difficult times as well—during times when we are more likely to question His nearness. He says in Isaiah 43:2,

> When you pass through the waters,
>   I will be with you;
> and when you pass through the rivers,
>   they will not sweep over you.
> When you walk through the fire,
>   you will not be burned;
>   the flames will not set you ablaze.

He doesn't promise that our lives will be free from difficulty. He does promise that we won't experience difficult times alone! God is saying, "Be strong and courageous. Do not be terrified; do not be discouraged, for the LORD your God will be with you wherever you go" (Josh. 1:9).

7

THE WORD OF GOD

It's the number-one best-selling book of all time. It was the first book to be printed, and it has been translated into more languages than any other written document. Within its covers are sixty-six books. They were written over a period of almost fifteen hundred years by more than forty authors from diverse backgrounds, occupations, and countries. This collection of books was written in three languages: Hebrew, Aramaic, and Greek. Most of its writers never knew each other, yet the entire work is connected by one great theme and central figure—Jesus Christ.

Unusual? Yes! That book, of course, is the Bible—the Word of God. Its construction would be totally impossible unless the Bible had a single author, and it did: the Holy Spirit of God. The Bible is the only book in which God has chosen to reveal Himself to the world. It is absolutely true, completely trustworthy, and the most relevant book you will ever read: "All Scripture is God–breathed and is useful for teaching, rebuking, correcting and training in righteousness, so that the man of God may be thoroughly equipped for every good work" (2 Tim. 3:16–17).

Dr. John R. W. Stott explained, "Not that God breathed into

the writers, nor that He somehow breathed into the writings to give them their special character, but . . . what was written by men was breathed out by God. He spoke through them. They were His spokesmen."[1]

THE POWER OF THE WORD

God has equipped you with a powerful instrument for spiritual battle, "The sword of the Spirit, which is the Word of God" (Eph. 6:17). God's Spirit uses the Word of God to accomplish His work.

Dr. A. W. Tozer said, "The great need of the hour among persons spiritually hungry is twofold: first, to know the Scriptures, apart from which no saving truth will be vouchsafed by our Lord; the second, to be enlightened by the Spirit, apart from Whom the Scriptures will not be understood."[2]

A WEAPON

In Ephesians 6, the Word of God is called a sword. The Bible is powerful and fearful to many people.

I made my first trip behind the Iron Curtain to Communist Romania in 1988. My weeks there were enlightening in many ways. A friend who had often traveled through Eastern Europe briefed me on what to expect. But I still had questions, and I was somewhat apprehensive. He advised me to leave my personal Bible at a hotel in Vienna, Austria, before I crossed into Communist Hungary. I could pick up my Bible on the return trip. Once I had crossed the border and reached my destination, I was to borrow a Bible from a Romanian pastor.

In Vienna, I met a friend from Texas who had visited Romania once before. He was to travel with me to meet our contacts in Romania. We spent ten hours driving across Hungary and finally arrived at the Romanian border. I vividly remember the feeling of apprehension as we drove up to the border crossing on that cold January afternoon. The scene reminded me of a World War II movie. But it was much worse because it was reality. It was cold and snowing, and armed guards were everywhere I looked.

I am still amazed at the first question the guard asked when he examined my passport: "Do you have a Bible?"

Why would an entire country fear the Bible? Not until he was ready to search our van and baggage did the guard ask, "Do you have pornography? Do you have arms or ammunition? Do you have drugs?"

We made it safely across the border and to the city of Oradea. Throughout that first trip and the many others I have made to Romania, I witnessed firsthand the power of God. Romania was one of the most repressive Communist countries in the Eastern Bloc. In the midst of persecution and desperate need, the Romanian church stood strong through prayer. It was my joy, honor, and privilege to see God's mighty hand work through His people even in the face of tremendous opposition and difficulty. It is the closest thing I have experienced to what I believe the Wesley revival was like in England. Romania is not the first nation brought to her knees by the power of God's Word. Even secular historians credit the Wesley revival for saving England from an upheaval like the violent French Revolution. Where the Word of God is preached in the power of the Holy Spirit, the sword of the Spirit is a powerful weapon to protect and bring justice.

LIFE-CHANGING POWER

I am thankful for my many friends in Romania. I am a stronger servant of the Lord today because of their investments in my life. One of those friends is a young evangelist named John. Before the revolution, John was an official in Romania's Young Communist Party. He was second in command only to the dictator Nicolae Ceausescu's son Nicki. One day as John and I were talking, I asked how he came to Christ. His amazing story demonstrates the power of the Word of God.

The Communist Party gave John a Bible. Yes—you read that correctly. The Communist Party of Romania gave him a Bible to study so that he could refute "weak-minded Christians." Well, you guessed it! God's Spirit began to work in John's life as he read the Word of God. John prayed to receive Christ as his Savior. I still get excited thinking about the pure power of God's Word working in John's life.

I asked John, "What did you do then?" Without any hesitation he said, "I did what I had to—I told the Communist Party what I had done." The party officials told John to think about it and come back later. "I do not need to think about it! I have given my life to Christ!" he replied.

John was imprisoned in a work camp where he was forced to do hard labor. Each day as he worked in the hot summer sun or the winter's extreme cold, the Communist leaders ridiculed and mocked him because of his faith. They told John he had lost his mind. He was later banished from the country to do hard labor in Cuba. John was returned to Romania and reunited with his family just prior to the Romanian revolution.

I believe that the international secular press never fully reported what God did in Romania during the revolution. In its conception, the revolution was totally Christian. As my friend Peter Dugulescu, pastor of First Baptist Church in Timisoara, says, "How can you call it a 'revolution'? In a revolution you have two sides fighting with weapons of war. The Communist authorities had an army, guns, tanks, and ammunition. All we had was the Word of God, His Spirit, prayers, and songs. And we won! That was not a revolution. It was a miracle."

The Word of God is powerful! "For the Word of God is living and active. Sharper than any doubled-edged sword, it penetrates even to dividing soul and spirit, joints and marrow; it judges the thoughts and attitudes of the heart. Nothing in all creation is hidden from God's sight. Everything is uncovered and laid bare before the eyes of Him to whom we must give an account" (Heb. 4:12–13).

GOD'S MESSAGE TO YOU

What makes the Bible so unusual? Why is it so popular? It is not merely a book of wisdom and history. The distinguishing characteristic of the Bible is that it is God's personal communication to you. The poet in Psalms wrote that God's scriptures "are my delight; they are my counselors" (Ps. 119:24). God breathed (inspired) the Bible in the hearts and minds of the men and women who penned its words. God assured the prophet Jeremiah, "I have put My words in your mouth" (Jer. 1:9). God told the prophet Ezekiel, "You must speak My words to them" (Ezek. 2:7). King David declared, "The Spirit of the LORD spoke through me; His Word was on my tongue" (2 Sam. 23:2).

The Bible is divided into two major sections: the Old Testament and the New Testament. The word *testament* means agreement—it is God's agreement with His creation to provide a plan of salvation and communication.

GOD IS THE AUTHOR

The Bible is relevant to today's culture because its message comes from an eternal source: God. Since God is eternal, transcending all time dimensions, His Word is eternal. The psalmist proclaimed,

> Your Word, O LORD, is eternal;
>> it stands firm in the heavens.
> Your faithfulness continues through all generations;
>> you established the earth, and it endures. (Ps. 119:89–90)

Even though the human writers of the Bible lived thousands of years before us in a part of the world many of us have never seen, the content of the Bible speaks to the core issues of our lives. We have changed, along with our culture, but God remains the same. God has no need to change because He is complete, and every development and change on earth originates with Him as Creator. His Word is eternally relevant to us and eternally personal.

> God is not a man, that He should lie,
>> nor a son of man, that He should change His mind.
> Does He speak and then not act?
>> Does He promise and not fulfill? (Num. 23:19)

Dr. John R. W. Stott addressed the issue of God's authority: "If it is a word from God, it has authority over men. For behind every word that anybody utters stands the person who speaks it.

It is the speaker himself (his character, knowledge, and position) who determines how people regard his words. So God's Word carries God's authority. It is because of who He is that we believe what He has said."[3]

The Bible exists to reveal God to you. His personality, His provision, and His promises are at your fingertips. When you open His Word, you open a personal word of instruction for living a successful, peaceful, and holy life: "The unfolding of [God's] words gives light; it gives understanding to the simple" (Ps. 119:130). As you read and study the Bible, you have the resources available to become mature in your faith and to develop a closer relationship with God. It is your necessary equipment in your spiritual journey. "All Scripture is God-breathed and is useful for teaching, rebuking, correcting and training in righteousness, so that the man of God may be thoroughly equipped for every good work" (2 Tim. 3:16–17). The great preacher and Bible teacher Dr. Charles Haddon Spurgeon wrote, "A man who has his Bible at his fingers' ends, and in his heart's core, is a champion in any conflict."

THE IMPORTANCE OF GOD'S WORD

Revelation of God's Character

The Word of God is important, first of all, because it reveals the character of God to us. Because we are human, we have a limited knowledge of God. His thoughts and His ways are far beyond our comprehension. But God, in mercy and love, has allowed us to glimpse His greatness. He has given us His Word to reveal things about Him that we can understand in our finite minds. Through the Bible, we not only know about God intellectually, we come to know God personally.

From the first book in the Bible, Genesis, to the last book of Revelation, God is continually revealing His character to us. Each glimpse brings us closer to understanding His redeeming plan for our lives. As you read the Bible, ask, *What does this scripture teach me about God?*

For example, God's Word reveals His absolute love for you: "May Your unfailing love be my comfort, according to Your promise" (Ps. 119:76). Throughout His Word, God has placed beautiful reminders of His commitment to you. One outstanding reminder is the account of His sacrificial death at Calvary. As you read the account of Christ's crucifixion (John 18–19), you see a graphic display of God's love for you. It is a love so great that it offers God's dearest possession (His only Son, Jesus) to pay the penalty for your sin. His Word explains that Christ's death in your place was the only way you could be forgiven of sin.

Instructions for Daily Living

The Word of God is important because it teaches you how to live. "Your Word is a lamp to my feet," wrote the psalmist (Ps. 119:105). The Bible is a Guidebook—a divine "Owner's Manual" for your life. In His Word, God has given you everything you need to know about living a whole and satisfying life. The Apostle Peter explained, "[God's] divine power has given us everything we need for life and godliness through our knowledge of Him Who called us by His own glory and goodness" (2 Peter 1:3).

The Bible does not detail how you should deal with every single circumstance in life but it gives you basic principles that you can apply to any situation. God has not supplied a moment-by-moment guide to decision-making in your life. He never mentions when you should continue your education, where you should work, or how much you should spend on a house. But through His words, He teaches you the type of attitude you should have and the issues you should consider when you face those demands. Neither does the Bible tell you with whom to connect but it does teach you how to build wholesome relationships and warns you about relationships that keep you from living in holiness and contentment. The Bible is not a magic book to help you achieve financial prosperity, but it teaches principles of integrity and discipline that will contribute to your success—financially and otherwise. The Bible is the most valuable guide for your journey of life.

Instructions for Holy Living

God has also revealed His standard for spiritual integrity, and has provided a resource for meeting that standard. The psalmist asked, "How can a young man keep his way pure? By living according to Your Word" (Ps. 119:9). God doesn't "lower the bar" to accommodate our weakness. He offers us the wisdom and motivation to help us reach His expectations through His infallible instruction.

The Bible not only defines those attitudes and actions that result in sin (disobedience against God), it teaches you how to avoid them. Its advice is invaluable when it comes to living a spiritually peaceful life. Thus, reading and studying God's Word are not optional for a Christian. You cannot be an effective follower of the Lord Jesus Christ without a regular encounter with Him through His Word.

THE WORD OF GOD IS TRUSTWORTHY

We live in an age when even our most trusted institutions have become suspect. The walls of our scientific, historical, political, and ethical establishments have either cracked or crumbled. Perhaps you are wondering whether the Bible is really trustworthy. The answer is an unequivocal yes! "The statutes You have laid down are righteous; they are fully trustworthy" (Ps. 119:138). You can completely trust the Bible. After all, if you are going to model your life after this Book and use it as your primary source for getting to know the God of the universe, you need to be sure that you can trust it. Both internal and external evidence point to the authenticity of the Bible. Internal evidence is found within the Bible. External evidence includes outside proofs not taken from the Bible.

Internal Evidence

I mentioned earlier that forty people wrote the Bible. Some may say that having so many authors jeopardizes the Bible's validity, but this is one of the most remarkable signs of God's direction. The Bible has one unique theme that continually surfaces: salvation, God's desire and plan to be in a redemptive relationship with humanity. The Bible's writers penned their words not knowing they would eventually be in the canon (authorized biblical writings) of Scripture. Most of the writers did not know each other or live in the same times. It was absolutely impossible for them to collaborate or create a unified book that continually portrays a similar view of God and His plan for His creation. Yet that's precisely what the Bible is.

Prophecy is another significant proof of the Bible's truth. We read in Deuteronomy 18:21–22, "'How can we know when a message has not been spoken by the LORD?' If what a prophet proclaims in the name of the LORD does not take place or come true, that is a message the LORD has not spoken." Hundreds of years later, the apostle Peter wrote, "Prophecy never had its origin in the will of man, but men spoke from God as they were carried along by the Holy Spirit" (2 Peter 1:21).

Furthermore, the Bible records the fulfillment of its own prophecies. Many Old Testament prophecies are fulfilled in the New Testament, for example, the extensive prophecies about Jesus' birth, life, and sacrificial death in the book of Isaiah. Isaiah prophesied the birth of Jesus:

> For to us a Child is born,
> > to us a Son is given,
> > and the government will be on His shoulders.
> And He will be called
> > Wonderful Counselor, Mighty God,
> > Everlasting Father, Prince of Peace.
> Of the increase of His government and peace
> > there will be no end.
> He will reign on David's throne
> > and over His kingdom,
> > establishing and upholding it
> > with justice and righteousness
> > from that time on and forever.
> The zeal of the LORD Almighty
> > will accomplish this. (Isa. 9:6–7)

Isaiah specified how the wonderful event would happen: "Therefore the Lord Himself will give you a sign: The virgin will be with child and will give birth to a Son, and will call Him Immanuel" (Isa. 7:14). (*Immanuel* means "God with us.") The promise of spiritual deliverance in the form of a Person miraculously sent from God was given in the first book of the Bible

(Gen. 3:15). Isaiah continued the theme hundreds of years later. And again, God is revealed to be personally involved with our spiritual freedom.

Micah, another Old Testament prophet, pinpointed the place of Jesus' birth:

> But you, Bethlehem Ephrathah,
>> though you are small among the clans of Judah,
> out of you will come for Me
>> One who will be ruler over Israel,
> whose origins are from of old,
>> from ancient times. (Mic. 5:2)

Those prophecies are fulfilled in the New Testament:

> So Joseph also went up from the town of Nazareth in Galilee to Judea, to Bethlehem the town of David, because he belonged to the house and line of David. He went there to register with Mary, who was pledged to be married to him and was expecting a child. While they were there, the time came for the baby to be born, and she gave birth to her firstborn, a son. She wrapped Him in cloths and placed Him in a manger, because there was no room for them in the inn. And there were shepherds living out in the fields nearby, keeping watch over their flocks at night. An angel of the Lord appeared to them, and the glory of the Lord shone around them, and they were terrified. But the angel said to them, "Do not be afraid. I bring you good news of great joy that will be for all the people. Today in the town of David a Savior has been born to you; He is Christ the Lord." (Luke 2:4–11)

From His kingly lineage to His exemplary life, Isaiah vividly portrayed the childhood and adult ministry of the Lord Jesus Christ:

> A shoot will come up from the stump of Jesse;
>   from His roots a Branch will bear fruit.
> The Spirit of the LORD will rest on Him—
>   the Spirit of wisdom and of understanding,
>   the Spirit of counsel and of power,
>   the Spirit of knowledge and of the fear of the LORD—
> and He will delight in the fear of the LORD . . .
> Righteousness will be His belt
>   and faithfulness the sash around His waist. (Isa. 11:1–3, 5)

The New Testament historian tells us how that prophecy was fulfilled in Jesus' exemplary life: "Jesus grew in wisdom and stature, and in favor with God and men" (Luke 2:52).

Isaiah also prophesied that Jesus would die a sacrificial death:

> But He was pierced for our transgressions,
>   He was crushed for our iniquities;
> the punishment that brought us peace was upon Him,
>   and by His wounds we are healed. (Isa. 53:5)

These words, probably mysterious to the listeners in Isaiah's day, are clearly fulfilled through Christ. The apostle John wrote of that prophecy's fulfillment:

> One of the soldiers pierced Jesus' side with a spear, bringing a sudden flow of blood and water. The man who saw it has given testimony, and his testimony is true. He knows that he tells the truth, and he testifies so that you also may believe.

These things happened so that the scripture would be fulfilled:
"Not one of His bones will be broken," and, as another scrip
ture says, "They will look on the one they have pierced."
(John 19:34–36)

Jesus specifically intended to fulfill prophecy. He said, "Do not
think that I have come to abolish the Law or the Prophets; I have
not come to abolish them but to fulfill them" (Matt. 5:17). Jesus
affirmed the validity of biblical prophecy in the Old Testament
and testified to the unity of Scripture.

External Evidence

The Bible is also qualified by external sources. Many archae-
ological sites testify to the Bible's authenticity. Excavations show
that Babylon, the place of the Jewish captivity, was indeed a powerful and splendid city. But living during the high point of the
city's cultural and political dominance, Isaiah, Jeremiah, and
Daniel prophesied that Babylon would be ruined. In 538 B.C.,
those prophecies were fulfilled. Excavations have uncovered a
series of tablets written in Babylon that confirm the events
described in 2 Kings 24:15. Other biblical sites such as Athens,
Jericho, Jerusalem, Susa, and Ur have been excavated extensively
and fit precisely with history as recorded in the Bible.

Furthermore, political documents and royal records from
other countries at the time of Jerusalem have been found that
include information about the Jews. For example, archaeologists
have uncovered many accounts of the worldwide flood in Noah's
time. These testimonies fit the Bible's.

The Bible's internal evidence and external evidence are tight
and flawless. The Bible does not contradict itself; it is a unified
Book with a common theme of humanity's redemption. God

gave you a trustworthy record of His character, His actions in history, and His promises for the future. As you become familiar with God's Word, you will see that it contains the Good News of Christ's redemption for the world, and it is God's personal communication of His character and of His plan for your life.

Your perspective on Scripture is vitally important. I have heard intelligent people say, "The Bible contains the Word of God." That may sound okay at first, but it is an incorrect and dangerous statement. It implies that some of the Bible is the Word of God, and some of it is not. If that is our belief system, how do we determine which portions are God's Word? Perhaps the happy psalms of praise are from God, but not the difficult command to "love your neighbor as yourself." When sinful humanity determines what is God's Word, we are in a dangerous situation.

Also, the Bible itself claims that it is completely true: "All Scripture is God-breathed and is useful for teaching, rebuking, correcting and training in righteousness" (2 Tim. 3:16). If we choose to disregard a portion of the Bible, we make its claim to truth a lie. Then how can we trust any of it? The Bible not only contains the Word of God; it is the Word of God!

I pray that you and I never face persecution. But even as you read these words, Christians in various parts of the world are being tortured and ridiculed for their faith. In fact, we live in the bloodiest era of human history, and martyrs dying for their faith in Christ have shed much of the blood.

What would you do if obedience to God's Word threatened your job, your possessions, your future, your family, and your life? What would you do if armed guards appeared and burst into your house, demanding, "Do you have any Bibles in this house?" Would you remain loyal to His Word? How would you decide what to do?

I read a story recently that shook me to the core. As tears ran down my cheeks, I prayed, "Lord, may I have the strength and courage to remain strong if I am ever challenged in this way." This true story is about a young teenage girl living in a Communist country. She was at a house church meeting with a small group of believers studying God's Word. Suddenly the doors burst open, and Communist authorities stormed into the room. Each person at the Bible study was physically and verbally abused. The people were then lined up against the wall, and a Bible was thrown in the middle of the room between them and the door.

The officer in charge said that anyone who wanted to leave could do so. All he needed to do was walk to the Bible, spit on it, and walk out. One at a time, three people walked to the Bible, spit on it, and walked out. Then the teenage girl walked to the Bible. With tears running down her cheeks she knelt down and picked up the Bible. She took her skirt, wiped off the spit, and then kissed the Bible. She wrapped her arms around the Bible, held it to her chest, and began to pray for the authorities. The officer in charge pulled out his gun and killed her.

During the past twelve years, I have had many opportunities to minister in the former Soviet bloc countries of Romania, the Ukraine, and Moldova. I have met hundreds of godly men and women who have paid dearly because of their faith in Christ and obedience to His Word. I thank God for the example they have been to me, demonstrating how to always stand strong, regardless of the consequences. They have taught me through their actions—much more than just a theological concept.

As a believer, I always have two good options: life and death. That may be a new thought for you, but it is a wonderful truth. The apostle Paul was living in that reality when he wrote from a

Roman prison, "For to me, to live is Christ, and to die is gain" (Phil. 1:21 NKJV).

THE ADVENTURE OF GOD'S WORD

Reading the Bible is a great adventure. Not only is God's Word filled with stories that would match any novel in exciting plots and subplots, but its language is exquisite and its historical accounts are flawless. But far beyond its literary excellence, the Bible is a personal letter of instruction and affirmation to you from God.

8

THE IMPORTANCE OF PRAYER

A football player is wheeled from the stadium on a stretcher. The TV commentator says, "I'm sure our prayers are with him." Your best friend tells you about her brother facing a life-threatening surgery, and you respond, "I'll be praying." The courts of the United States have sought to ban prayer from the public forum, but their verdicts are in vain. I love what former United States President Ronald Reagan said about school prayer: "As long as there are exams, no court will ever be able to stop prayer in school." Talking to God about life's concerns is almost as common as talking with others about the latest weather.

Nearly all religions engage in some form of prayer—reciting written prayers, singing or chanting prayers, meditating, and more. Some religions require followers to participate in mandatory prayer sessions, sometimes multiple times a day. For the Christian, however, prayer is somewhat different.

Whereas members of some religions pray to a variety of gods, Christians pray to one God—Jehovah. We do not have a set number of daily prayers or a required regimen. Followers of Christ believe that the Lord of the universe is available twenty-four hours per day to hear the prayers of His people. He graciously allows us to communicate with Him through prayer.

Because so many forms of prayer exist, many people are confused about what prayer really is. Prayer is not merely saying words to an invisible being. It is not just a ritual to be performed a certain number of times per day or before every meal. Prayer is a two-way conversation with a living God—both *talking* and *listening* to Him as you would with your best friend.

For the Christian, praying is an expression of love. Just as a loved one communicates words of devotion and affection, Christians express their adoration and allegiance to God in prayer. Prayer may be speaking out loud to Him, or it may take the form of silent thoughts. By quietly meditating about God, we can tune out distractions and focus on Him. Listening is also a significant part of prayer time. During those times of prayerful meditation, He will often place thoughts or phrases into the mind. At other times, God will speak to us through His Word, causing us to remember a verse from the Bible that we have heard, read, studied, or memorized. Conversation with God is our link to Him.

JESUS MODELED THE IMPORTANCE OF PRAYER

Though Jesus is God, when He chose to come to Earth, He took on the body and physical limitations of a human. During His ministry, Jesus depended on His heavenly Father. Often, He paused during a heavy schedule and spent time in conversation with God the Father. Luke recorded one such occasion: "It came to pass in those days that He went out to the mountain to pray, and continued all night in prayer to God" (Luke 6:12 NKJV).

His grueling schedule and the demands upon His life and ministry were burdens that Jesus gladly shared with His Father. Those prayer times brought affirmation and refreshment to the Savior. There, He could affirm His ministry focus.

Jesus . . . looked toward heaven and prayed: "Father, the time has come. Glorify your Son, that your Son may glorify You. For You granted Him authority over all people that He might give eternal life to all those You have given Him. Now this is eternal life: that they may know You, the only true God, and Jesus Christ, whom You have sent. I have brought You glory on earth by completing the work You gave Me to do." (John 17:1–4)

Through prayer, Jesus could express and accept the affection that existed between the heavenly Father and His Son. There, He could talk about the daily struggles and victories with Someone who really cared about Him. Many of those around Jesus cared only about His miracles. They sought Him out for the things He could do for them. Jesus understood that—and even welcomed it—but He needed to talk with the One who cared about Him, no strings attached.

Jesus prayed daily. Sometimes He prayed in an organized setting, such as the Jewish temple. Sometimes He prayed alone in a natural setting, in quiet solitude: "In the morning, having risen a long while before daylight, He went out and departed to a solitary place; and there He prayed" (Mark 1:35 NKJV). At other times, He gathered His followers around Him in an informal prayer group: "[Jesus] took Peter, John, and James and went up on the mountain to pray" (Luke 9:28 NKJV).

Prayer was an integral part of His earthly ministry: "Then little children were brought to Jesus for Him to place His hands on them and pray for them" (Matt. 19:13). Once, Jesus ministered privately to a disciple named Simon Peter and reminded him that He was taking Simon's concerns to His heavenly Father in prayer: "I have prayed for you, Simon, that your faith may not fail" (Luke 22:32). Jesus was a Man of prayer.

As He faced the most difficult hours of His life—the hours preceding His death on the cross—He retreated to one of His favorite places to pray, the Garden of Gethsemane. It is a beautiful olive grove on the Mount of Olives, just outside the city of Jerusalem. There He spent time in intense prayer.

> Then Jesus went with His disciples to a place called Gethsemane, and He said to them, "Sit here while I go over there and pray." He took Peter and the two sons of Zebedee along with him, and He began to be sorrowful and troubled. Then He said to them, "My soul is overwhelmed with sorrow to the point of death. Stay here and keep watch with Me." Going a little farther, He fell with His face to the ground and prayed, "My Father, if it is possible, may this cup be taken from Me. Yet not as I will, but as You will." (Matt. 26:36–39)

JESUS TAUGHT HIS FOLLOWERS HOW TO PRAY

His disciples watched in awe as Jesus communicated freely and lovingly with His heavenly Father. They saw firsthand the power of prayer. They wanted personal instruction in developing their prayer lives: "One day Jesus was praying in a certain place. When He finished, one of His disciples said to Him, 'Lord, teach us to pray'" (Luke 11:1). In response, the Son of God gave one of the most stirring seminars on prayer in all of history. And we all have the opportunity to share in it.

The disciple Matthew recorded this account of Jesus' teaching:

> "This, then, is how you should pray:
> 'Our Father in heaven,

hallowed be Your name,

Your kingdom come,

Your will be done on earth as it is in heaven.

Give us today our daily bread.

Forgive us our debts,

as we also have forgiven our debtors.

And lead us not into temptation,

but deliver us from the evil one.

Just as there are many ways to have a conversation with a person, so there are many ways to pray. Jesus instructed the disciples and us about what to include in our prayers.

ADORING GOD

Jesus began His prayer by addressing God: "Our Father in heaven, hallowed be Your name" (Matt. 6:9). *Hallowed* in this case means "holy" and "set apart." Jesus began His prayer by adoring God—immediately drawing attention to God and focusing on Him. Adoration of God through prayer is something that you can cultivate, even though it may not come naturally at first.

It may help to think of the way you praise a friend or teammate for a job well done. You focus completely on that person both for what he has done and for who he is. "You were incredible!" "You are always so thoughtful and generous."

Of course, when you praise the God of the universe, you're taking things to a whole new level. You can pray prayers of adoration by talking lovingly and reverently about God. Describe His character. Tell God what you like about Him, and elaborate on His personality traits. God has revealed His character to you through His Word, the Bible, and prayers of adoration are opportunities for you to reflect on and tell Him of His characteristics that you have been learning about and appreciating.

When Jesus began His prayer with adoration, He communicated to us: "God is supreme. He is worthy of your deepest respect. He deserves your attention." Praying prayers of adoration may be stretching for you at first, but the more you practice, the easier it will become.

I often use a hymn or a chapter from the book of Psalms. You may want to choose a song of praise to use as your prayer of adoration. Rather than sing it to God, read it as a prayer. A hymnbook can be a key aid to your prayer life. You can purchase one at your local Christian bookstore. In the index of most hymnals, the songs are arranged in several categories: author, composer, alphabetical, and topical. Under the topical section, you will find a subsection on adoration. A good one to start with is "All Hail the Power of Jesus' Name" by Rev. Edward Perronet:

> All hail the power of Jesus' name!
> Let angels prostrate fall;
> Bring forth the royal diadem,
> And crown Him Lord of all.
>
> Ye chosen seed of Israel's race,
> Ye ransomed from the fall,
> Hail Him who saves you by His grace,
> And crown Him Lord of all.
>
> Sinners, whose love can never forget
> The wormwood and the gall,
> Go spread your trophies at His feet,
> And crown Him Lord of all.

Let every kindred, every tribe,
On this terrestrial ball,
To Him all majesty ascribe,
And crown Him Lord of all.

O that with yonder sacred throng
We at His feet will fall!
We'll join the everlasting song,
And crown Him Lord of all.

Always remember that prayer is far more than just asking for things from God. Primarily, prayer is enjoying the presence of God. The more time you spend getting to know Him, the richer your prayer life will be. Asking is definitely part of prayer. But I have discovered that the more time I spend in worship and adoration, the more power I have in my prayer life.

ALIGNING WITH GOD

Jesus continued His prayer, as well as His lesson, "Your kingdom come, Your will be done on earth as it is in heaven" (Matt. 6:10). This sentence demonstrates Jesus' alignment with the Father. Jesus knows that human beings often want something different from what God wants. He understands that we often want to be in full control of our lives. The apostle Paul addressed the problem in his letter to Christians at Rome: "In my inner being I delight in God's law; but I see another law at work in the members of my body, waging war against the law of my mind and making me a prisoner of the law of sin at work within my members" (Rom. 7:22–23).

When we pray, we seek to align our will with God's will. In Matthew 6:10, Jesus said He wanted God's kingdom to come and God's will to be done. In other words, He wanted God's purpose to be accomplished on earth just as God's purpose is carried out in heaven—completely.

As you grow in your spiritual journey, you will learn that Christians sometimes pray for things that God does not want to give to us—at least not yet. Prayer is an activity that changes *you*. It helps you to conform to God's perfect plan for your life.

Jesus did not want to die on the cross. He had no human desire to suffer such an agonizing and humiliating death, but He desired to do His heavenly Father's will more than anything.

He could have asked His Father to spare Him from death. But that would not have fit into God's plan to bring forgiveness and acceptance through the offering of His Son. Instead of demanding deliverance, Jesus prayed, "My Father, if it is possible, may this cup be taken from Me. Yet not as I will, but as You will" (Matt. 26:39). Praying to be in alignment with God changes the way you look at the situations in your life.

How is your prayer life? Are you praying according to the will of God? There are times when we do not know how to pray in the will of God, so we say, "Lord, Your will be done." There are other times when we can pray with boldness because we know we are praying the heart-cry of God Himself.

ASKING GOD

After Jesus aligned Himself with God's will, He made a request: "Give us today our daily bread" (Matt. 6:11). It was the asking part of Jesus' prayer. Jesus showed the disciples that they were to ask God to provide for them. In prayer, Jesus acknowledged that His heavenly Father has the power and authority to meet His needs—including physical, financial, and social needs.

By asking for God's supply, we demonstrate our dependence on and trust in Him. James the apostle wrote, "You do not have, because you do not ask God" (James 4:2). He continued, "Confess your sins to each other and pray for each other so that you may be healed. The prayer of a righteous man is powerful and effective" (5:16).

As Dr. Bill Bright said, "Why would we ask so little of such a great God?" God wants us to depend upon Him to meet our daily needs. Are you depending on Him in this area of your life? I do not have any concrete evidence, but I firmly believe that a great hindrance to prayer in North America is that we have all the material things we need and more. Most of us don't really *need* to pray about where our next meal is coming from. We have money in the bank and plenty of food at home. If we run out, it's just a quick trip to one of many grocery stores near the house. It takes a conscious effort to remind ourselves that we are totally dependent upon God.

The first time I went to Romania was January 1988. Food lines were a way of life for Romanians. They waited in line for everything. One line for milk, another for eggs, one for bread, and up to a six-hour wait for a piece of meat. I asked my friend Rev. Eugene Grosa, "Eugene, how difficult is it for you to get meat in Romania?" He replied, "Meat, what is that?" Yes, he was being facetious. But I quickly realized that my brothers and sisters in Romania were put in a position of total dependence on God. Through the Romanian church, God often reiterated two key lessons for my life: prayer and faith.

In reality, all of us are totally dependent upon God. We in the Western world have the challenge of reminding ourselves of this reality. Our challenge is not to allow the god of materialism to rob us of the joy and privilege of total dependence upon God our Provider. God alone is the One who can "give us today our daily bread."

Another aspect of asking is requesting God's activity and supply in the lives of others. This is called *intercessory prayer* (interceding on behalf of another—acting as a go-between). Praying for others is active and difficult work. It requires time and perseverance. But your prayer acts to release God's power in the lives of others. Intercessory prayer is a way of serving others, and God delights to hear the requests of a person aligned with Him and intent on serving Him.

ACKNOWLEDGING GOD

After Jesus prayed for God to provide for physical needs, He asked God to meet His spiritual needs. It is a prayer of acknowledgment—acknowledging that God is the supreme authority over every area of our lives: "Forgive us our debts, as we also have forgiven our debtors" (Matt. 6:12). *Debts* refers not to financial debts, but to spiritual debts. There are many areas of our lives in which we should acknowledge God's supreme authority and supply.

1. We Acknowledge Our Dependence on His Mercy and Forgiveness

Jesus Himself had no spiritual debt. He is the only person who ever lived a sinless life on earth: "For we do not have a high priest who is unable to sympathize with our weaknesses, but we have One [Jesus] who has been tempted in every way, just as we are—yet was without sin" (Heb. 4:15). This portion of Jesus' prayer acknowledged His will to be reconciled with others and to be reconciled to His heavenly Father's will.

But we are not free from sin. Through these words, Jesus'

prayer taught the disciples and teaches us that when we have failed to measure up to God's perfect standards, we should acknowledge it (confess it). Our spiritual failures make us spiritually indebted to God. Confession is important because its very action is a step toward restoration with God.

The apostle John wrote, "If we confess our sins, [God] is faithful and just and will forgive us our sins and purify us from all unrighteousness" (1 John 1:9). It is not that God wants to hear us repeat our *faults*. Rather, He wants us to acknowledge our *faith*—that nothing or no one means more to us than He does. In the acknowledgement part of your prayer, you admit your sin and your need for restoration and fellowship with God. You agree with God about your needy spiritual state.

2. We Acknowledge That Without God's Power and Authority, We Are Helpless Against the Attacks of Our Spiritual Enemy, Satan

Jesus continued His example of prayer by saying, "And lead us not into temptation, but deliver us from the evil one" (Matt. 6:13). In this prayer for protection, Jesus showed us that we should ask God to defend us spiritually and to help us stand strong in the face of sin.

Once you have accepted Christ as the Lord of your life, Satan begins to attack you in a whole new way. He does this through evil thoughts, subtle reminders of the past, feelings of weakness and inferiority in your mind, and many trying circumstances. Satan will use any way he can to cause you to doubt God's acceptance of you and His perfect plan for your life. Jesus knows that His followers must be armed for spiritual battle.

You are spiritually weak on your own, but with God you have spiritual power to withstand the devil's temptations. Ask

God to protect you from sin and to help you resist temptation and choose pure paths. He is the only One who can enable you to overcome evil. "No temptation has seized you except what is common to man. And God is faithful; He will not let you be tempted beyond what you can bear. But when you are tempted, He will also provide a way out so that you can stand up under it" (1 Cor. 10:13).

3. We Acknowledge His Holy and Just Superiority

Jesus concluded His prayer model by saying, "Yours is the kingdom and the power and the glory forever. Amen" (Matt. 6:13 NKJV). Not only is this an example of thanking God for what He has done, but it demonstrates thanking Him for Who He is. God is supreme. He can supply supremely, protect supremely, and accept worship supremely. There is no one like Him—and no one above Him.

By ending our prayer with an acknowledgment of God's supreme authority, we affirm our faith in Him and our dependence on Him. We affirm that God is the Source of our forgiveness and acceptance. We affirm that He is our protection and hope for life beyond physical death. We affirm that everything we are and hope to be is included in His all-knowing, eternal plan for our lives.

Though Jesus gave us clear and concise instructions on prayer, we must not assume that prayer is an easy procedure. It's hard work. It takes disciplined practice. But God has promised His help: "The Spirit helps us in our weakness. We do not know what we ought to pray for, but the Spirit Himself intercedes for us with groans that words cannot express" (Rom. 8:26).

Like any meaningful conversation, prayer requires time and thoughtfulness. But it's the best conversation you will ever have, and it's the most important use of your time. Prayer is your connection to God. It is His way of communicating with you, and if you desire to grow in your relationship with Him, you need to cultivate the practice of prayer. We are told to "pray continually" in 1 Thessalonians 5:17. Similarly Ephesians 6:18 urges, "Pray in the Spirit on all occasions with all kinds of prayers and requests. With this in mind, be alert and always keep on praying for all the saints."

EXAMPLES OF ANSWERED PRAYERS

I struggled over sharing examples of answered prayer with you, but I believe that the Lord placed the desire in my heart. In obedience to His leading, I am going to describe some especially memorable direct answers to prayers. All glory for answered prayers belongs to the Lord. I have not scratched the surface of the power and potential in prayer, but I have experienced enough of His goodness to know that I want to see more. I have also seen enough of His power, goodness, and provision to make me wonder why I have not trusted Him for greater things. As I record these few examples of answered prayers, my heart is humbled before my loving Lord. He alone is worthy of all praise. I pray that these examples will be a peephole into the possibilities of prayer in your life and will cause you to want to go deeper in your walk with the Lord.

In 1981, we had just concluded an evangelistic crusade in the extreme southern part of Haiti one Sunday night. Our group of eight got up early Monday morning and loaded our VW bus for the return trip to the capital city of Port-au-Prince. We were to fly home later that morning. The luggage rack on top of the VW bus was packed high with our baggage and sound equipment. The mountain road was steep and narrow with treacherous hairpin curves. As we were driving through the mountains, our driver did not negotiate a curve, and the bus swerved off the road. We had been rounding a curve with no guardrail. Suddenly the bus was falling from the side of the mountain.

I heard at least two of us shout out loud in prayer, "Jesus, help!" Then it was as though the very hand of God reached out, caught the van, and set it on the mountain road again. We were in shock for a few moments. As we began to realize that we had just experienced a miracle and an answer to prayer, we stopped the van and worshiped our loving Lord, giving thanks and praise to Him for sparing our lives.

I cannot explain why God answered our prayer with that miracle, but I know He did. I know that many wonderful Christians, including several of my friends, have lost their lives in accidents. God could have intervened for them also but did not. These are unanswerable questions. We learn from the Bible,

> "For My thoughts are not your thoughts,
> neither are your ways My ways,"
> declares the LORD. (Isa. 55:8)

◆ ◆ ◆

One of my close friends is Karl Stoltzfus. He and I have been friends for almost thirty years, since we were in college together. Karl is chairman of the Board of Directors for Wingfield Ministries. He has a multifaceted aviation business, and he is an excellent pilot. Part of his business involves major spraying operations for medflies, mosquitoes, and other insects.

One morning while I was praying, I felt especially impressed to pray for Karl. Later that day I sent him a note with several Bible promises. I mentioned in my note that I was praying for him. Karl received the note the next day, read it, and placed it in his Bible. He then went out to the loaded plane to pilot a large spraying job. Just after liftoff, a large bird hit the windshield of his plane on the copilot's side. The windshield shattered, and glass and bird remains were strewn all over the cockpit. There was no copilot on that flight, and Karl was able to land the plane with no injury. I firmly believe that I was prompted by the Holy Spirit to pray for my friend's emergency situation.

◆ ◆ ◆

The summer of 1990 following the overthrow of the communist regime in Romania, a number of Romanian church leaders invited me to return to the country for a preaching mission in four cities. These cities had never had the privilege of an evangelistic outreach, and I was excited to see what God would do. Our ministry team held four Encounters, citywide evangelistic outreaches sponsored by the local churches. I will long remember the first night in Timisoara. I was preaching the gospel in a stadium that had been built to promote and proclaim communism. When I gave the invitation following the message, I thought my translator, Peter, had misinterpreted what I had said and dismissed the crowd. It seemed as though everyone got up to leave. I then realized the people were not leaving, they were responding to the invitation to accept Christ!

After several nights of rich harvests, we began evening meetings in the city of Medias. As I was preaching, a storm approached the stadium. The wind began to blow, and I could see a huge black cloud approaching. I knelt on the platform and prayed, "Lord God, there are people in this stadium who have never heard the gospel. They may never have another opportunity. I ask that You stay the storm and allow us to continue."

Several American businessmen in our ministry team were sitting in the top rows of the stadium that evening. They later reported that as the storm came to the stadium, it literally divided and went around the stadium. In the path of the storm, houses were destroyed, trees were uprooted, and power lines were downed. But in the stadium, we continued the service, and hundreds of people gave their lives to Christ that night. To God be all the glory!

Later in another city on that same trip, a huge rainstorm developed about a mile away from the soccer stadium where I was preaching. On the platform with me that night were Romanian pastors. As I preached the gospel to a standing-room-only crowd I could hear the pastors behind me praying. When I extended the invitation for people to respond to the gospel message, the response was overwhelming. People rushed to the front with tears streaming down their faces. The press of people trying to get down to the field to respond to the invitation was so great, some were climbing over the fence surrounding the track.

We finished counseling with all who responded to the invitation. We distributed the follow-up material and packed up the sound system. When the last person climbed into the van, rain began to pour. As we drove away, the team told me what had happened during the service as I preached. Three times, a huge cloud of pouring rain came to the edge of the stadium. As the rain cloud neared the stadium, the pastors prayed, asking God to hold off the storm. The black cloud moved back away from the stadium. And again, it began coming forward. When it came to the stadium's edge, once more the pastors prayed it away. This happened three times! Give God all the glory!

◆   ◆   ◆

Not all prayers have immediate answers. My parents prayed for one person every day for many years. As a young boy, I remember thinking, *Why are they praying for this man? Nothing has changed.* Several months after my dad went home to be with the Lord, this man gave his life to Christ.

There are many excellent books on prayer. I suggest you read *Power Through Prayer,* by E. M. Bounds—it's a classic. Another great book on prayer is *Praying the Lord's Prayer for Spiritual Breakthrough,* by Dr. Elmer Towns.

There is so much about prayer that I need to learn. I feel that I have only begun to understand the potential and work toward where I need to be in my prayer life. I know this for certain: the study of prayer is important, but do not spend most of your time studying and talking about prayer! The most important thing any of us can learn about prayer is, *just do it!*

9

THE NORMAL CHRISTIAN LIFE

arly in 2000, (PETA) People for the Ethical Treatment of Animals launched a campaign against milk. The "Got Beer?" campaign targeted universities, urging college students to "wipe off those milk mustaches and replace them with . . . foam." PETA claimed that research showed beer is actually better for people than milk. They gave away bottle openers saying, "Drinking Responsibly Means Not Drinking Milk."

Regardless of its calorie and fat content, no one has ever caused an auto accident or abused a spouse under the influence of milk! And I am thankful that PETA pulled the "Got Beer?" campaign almost immediately under the heavy pressure from Mothers Against Drunk Driving (MADD) and many others who were truly concerned for the health and lives of college students.[1] The New Testament doesn't address milk consumption, but the apostle Paul wrote to the Christians in the city of Ephesus: "Do not get drunk on wine, which leads to debauchery. Instead, be filled with the Spirit" (Eph. 5:18). This verse from God's Word gives two obvious commands. First, "do not get drunk." Second, "be filled with the Spirit."

A drunken person is under the influence or control of an intoxicating substance such as alcohol. Paul said that condition leads to *debauchery*, or "leading away from virtue or excellence." As Christians we are commanded not to be controlled by alcohol.

You probably aren't thinking, *I can hardly wait to put this book down so I can get drunk!* That would be absurd. We do not need to look far to see the wisdom of God's command, "Do not get drunk." Alcohol abuse is the leading cause of death on the highway. It has shattered families and ruined the dreams of countless young people. Its destruction might have touched your life at some level. You probably agree that the apostle's advice is sound.

As foolish as it would be for you to put down this book and get drunk, it would be even more absurd for you to stop reading without making certain that you are filled with the Holy Spirit. The Holy Spirit is one of God's greatest gifts! It is so central to His plan for you as a Christian that God commands you to "be filled with the Spirit."

Jesus promised to send the Holy Spirit as a "Counselor" to all believers (John 14:16). Note the Counselor is promised to all believers, not a select few. Some Christians, however, consider a Spirit-filled life to be out of the spiritual norm. They describe it as an abstract spiritual experience reserved for the spiritually elite—pastors, missionaries, or other church leaders. For many, the Spirit-filled life was relegated to the radical fringes of Christianity.

With all these opinions circulating, people have formed hundreds of philosophies on the Spirit-filled life. Some live in fear of what the Holy Spirit might do to them. Others associate sensational experiences with the Spirit-filled life, questioning their validity.

Despite all the confusion, the Christian life is the Spirit-filled life. Anything less is anemic Christianity at best. Set aside your preconceived notions and the impressions based on past experiences or hearsay to consider what God's Word says about the Holy Spirit. This study could revolutionize your Christian life and add unimaginable power to your spiritual journey.

CONFUSION ABOUT THE SPIRIT-FILLED LIFE

Why is there so much confusion about the Spirit-filled life? Because Satan fosters it. He hates the truth of the Bible and will do everything possible to keep people away from it. The gospel writer wrote about false teachers influenced by Satan, "You belong to your father, the devil, and you want to carry out your father's desire. He was a murderer from the beginning, not holding to the truth, for there is no truth in him. When he lies, he speaks his native language, for he is a liar and the father of lies" (John 8:44).

The Bible says that "God is not the author of confusion" (1 Cor. 14:33 NKJV). Obviously, if God *isn't* the author of confusion, someone else *is*. That "someone" is Satan, the enemy of your Christian faith.

He doesn't want you to experience the joy of living a victorious Christian life. He wants you to be intellectually confused and emotionally defeated. He wants to keep you in bondage. Satan desires to keep you from a greater spiritual dimension. If he can trap you in spiritual confusion on this issue and prevent you from becoming all God created you to be, he wins a major victory. But God wants you to succeed. The sacrificial gift of His only Son proves it: "He who did not spare His own Son, but gave Him up for us all—how will He not also, along with Him, graciously give us all things?" (Rom. 8:32).

The command is not to be "drunk on wine"—under the control of earthly forces and accompanying self-defeat. Instead, we are commanded to be "filled with the Spirit"—under the influence of God in spiritual victory and understanding. Paul reassured us, "We have not received the spirit of the world but the Spirit who is from God, that we may understand what God has freely given us" (1 Cor. 2:12).

WHAT DOES IT MEAN TO BE FILLED WITH THE HOLY SPIRIT?

I believe God inspired the apostle Paul to link these two commands for a specific reason. We understand that a person who is drunk is under the control of alcohol. Alcohol captivates, motivates, and activates the drunkard.

Paul said that in the same way, a Christian is to be filled with the Holy Spirit. To be filled with the Spirit, you must come under the control of the Holy Spirit. You are now captivated, motivated, and activated by Him. You are no longer in control. Instead, the Holy Spirit gives your life new meaning and direction. In one of my favorite Bible verses, Jesus said, "The thief comes only to steal and kill and destroy; I have come that they may have life, and have it to the full" (John 10:10). If this is to be a reality in your life, the Spirit-filled life is not an option—it's the normal Christian life.

NOT IN YOUR OWN STRENGTH

There have been all types of teachings on the subject of the Spirit-filled life. Some of it thrives on sensationalism and borders on the bizarre. Some philosophies are incorrect. I heard one speaker describe the Spirit-filled life like this: he stood behind a podium and held up a glass of water and a glass of milk. He said the milk represented "self" and the water represented the Holy Spirit. "In order to be filled with the Spirit," he said, "you must empty yourself of 'self.'" To illustrate his point, he emptied the glass of milk into a bowl and then refilled it with the glass of water.

The problem with that illustration is that it is not what the Bible teaches! I call it liquid theology. You cannot empty yourself of your "self." You would become a chronic introvert, focusing on all the negative aspects of your life rather than looking at God—the only One who can give you the strength to live victoriously. You cannot defeat sin in your life through your own strength. We all need a Power greater than ourselves. That is why God commands us to be filled with the Spirit.

If you do not become a spiritually defeated introvert, that liquid theology will make you a hypocrite. When you are futilely attempting to empty yourself of "self," you will probably be assuring everyone that all is well with you spiritually. But deep inside, you are growing more frustrated and discouraged. If you're playing this game, most people around you already know that all is not well! Spiritual defeat may be disguised for a time, but your fine, fantastic, and fabulous facade will soon crumble. That mask will slip off in the stress and strains of life. No one can live the victorious Christian life in his own strength.

SPIRIT OF CRISIS

There is still more confusion about the Spirit-filled life centering on crisis. Some teach that the Spirit-filled life is a crisis experience. They emphasize a specific time in the Christian's spiritual life. They are right in one sense: the experience of being Spirit-filled does begin in a specific time frame. It is one of the most important events in a Christian's life. But I choose not to call it a crisis experience for several reasons.

1. *Crisis* is defined as "a paroxysmal attack of pain, distress, or disordered function."[2] In our society, an oil spill may cause an environmental crisis, or a civil war may be a national crisis. To most of us, associating crisis with the Spirit-filled life suggests a negative and traumatic experience. But the Spirit-filled life is one of health and wholeness, not distress or disorder.

2. Since God created us uniquely, we respond to various situations in decidedly different ways. As I have already said, each of us has a God-given personality that determines much of how we respond to life in general. This uniqueness affects how we react to spiritual encounters in our lives. For example, if you are quiet and reserved prior to being filled with the Spirit, you will most likely be quiet and reserved after you are filled. Conversely if you are a boisterous extrovert before you are filled with the Spirit, you will probably retain those traits afterward.

To classify everyone who experiences the Spirit-filled life with one word—claiming that he has undergone a crisis—negates the fact that individuals experience the manifest Holy Spirit in unique ways that suit each personality. The apostle Paul said, "There are different kinds of working, but the same God works all of them in all men. Now to each one the manifestation of the Spirit is given for the common good" (1 Cor. 12:6–7).

I am sure you have heard that "opposites attract." Of course, that is true of magnets, but it is often true of people too. That's certainly the case with my wife, Barbara, and me. There is strength in the union of opposite abilities. But as opposites, we respond to situations and experiences differently. That does not make my way right and Barbara's wrong; they are simply different.

For instance, Barbara and I like to go to basketball games—especially our son's. However, if you judged how much fun we had at a game based on volume or dramatic expressions, I would always win. I get involved! There is no question about which team I am cheering for! Barbara sits beside me relatively quiet, but she's having fun. We just respond differently.

In the same way, different people respond differently to the Spirit-filled life. God made you uniquely you. As we learned from Psalm 139 earlier, God loves you so much that He designed you to be who you are—one of a kind! You do not need to fit into anyone's box. Just allow Him to be who He already is in you.

3. I have observed that when being Spirit-filled is called a crisis, people are encouraged to seek a religious experience rather than a dynamic relationship with God through His Holy Spirit. A religious experience can become a phony spiritual shortcut. In the first-century church during the ministry of the evangelist Philip, one man tried to buy the effects of being filled with the Spirit:

> Now for some time a man named Simon had practiced sorcery in the city and amazed all the people of Samaria. He boasted that he was someone great, and all the people, both high and low, gave him their attention and exclaimed, "This man is the divine power known as the Great Power." They followed him because he had amazed them for a long time with his magic. But when they believed Philip as he preached the good news of the kingdom of God and the name of Jesus Christ, they were baptized, both men and women. Simon himself believed and was baptized. And he followed Philip everywhere, astonished by the great signs and miracles he saw. When the apostles in Jerusalem heard that Samaria had accepted the word of God, they sent Peter and John to them. When they arrived, they

prayed for them that they might receive the Holy Spirit, because the Holy Spirit had not yet come upon any of them; they had simply been baptized into the name of the Lord Jesus. Then Peter and John placed their hands on them, and they received the Holy Spirit. When Simon saw that the Spirit was given at the laying on of the apostles' hands, he offered them money and said, "Give me also this ability so that everyone on whom I lay my hands may receive the Holy Spirit." Peter answered: "May your money perish with you, because you thought you could buy the gift of God with money!" (Acts 8:9–20)

Today's efforts to capitalize on religious experience may not blatantly involve money, but people still get distracted by personal power and recognition. And to God, efforts to pervert the purpose of His gifts are as serious as Peter said.

4. When being filled with the Holy Spirit is a crisis experience, Christians risk developing an attitude of "been there, done that." The normal Christian life is a life that says, "Yes, Lord. Yes Lord. Yes Lord," on a daily basis. This is not a one-time experience that you look back to. It is a dynamic way of life that you experience daily. As you understand more of who God is, your desire for Him increases. And as you understand more of who you are, you in turn give those parts of your life to Him. The normal Christian life is one of growth. The Bible points out, "Being confident of this, that He who began a good work in you will carry it on to completion until the day of Christ Jesus" (Phil. 1:6).

QUESTIONS ABOUT THE SPIRIT-FILLED LIFE

"What does the Bible say about the genuine experience of being filled with the Spirit?"

"How can I be filled with the Holy Spirit?"

These are vital questions that you're probably asking because they relate directly to your spiritual journey. God has answered them in His Word, the Bible. Remember that He is not the author of confusion. God does not ask you to experience something and then make it difficult to understand. If you are going to be Spirit-filled as a way of life, you need to understand several basic concepts.

1. Who Is the Holy Spirit?

The Holy Spirit is God. Three persons make up the Trinity: God the Father, God the Son, and God the Holy Spirit. Each person of the Trinity is equal in personality, power, and provision. Notice the three persons mentioned in these verses: "Who is it that overcomes the world? Only he who believes that Jesus is the Son of God. This is the One who came by water and blood—Jesus Christ. He did not come by water only, but by water and blood. And it is the [Holy] Spirit who testifies, because the Spirit is the truth. For there are three that testify: the Spirit, the water and the blood; and the three are in agreement" (1 John 5:5–8).

According to the Bible, the Holy Spirit is a person who wills, thinks, and speaks. He was present at the creation of the world: "Now the earth was formless and empty, darkness was over the surface of the deep, and the Spirit of God was hovering over the waters" (Gen. 1:2). He put His blessing and anointing on certain people and occasions during Old Testament times. Well-known Old Testament leaders such as Moses and lesser-known people such as the builders and designers of the Israelites' Tabernacle were filled with the Holy Spirit's power: "Then the LORD said to Moses, 'See, I have chosen Bezalel . . . and I have filled him with the Spirit of God, with skill, ability and knowledge in all kinds of crafts'" (Ex. 31:1–3).

2. Where Is the Holy Spirit Now?

When Jesus was symbolically baptized at the beginning of His earthly ministry, all three persons of the Trinity—including the Holy Spirit—were present: "As soon as Jesus was baptized, He went up out of the water. At that moment heaven was opened, and He saw the Spirit of God descending like a dove and lighting on Him. And a voice from heaven said, 'This is my Son, whom I love; with Him I am well pleased'" (Matt. 3:16–17).

At the end of Jesus' earthly ministry, He gave His followers a significant promise: "I will ask the Father, and He will give you another Counselor to be with you forever—the Spirit of truth. The world cannot accept Him, because it neither sees Him nor knows Him. But you know Him, for He lives with you and will be in you. I will not leave you as orphans" (John 14:16–18).

Jesus promised to send His Spirit to His followers to continue His ministry through them: "You will receive power when the Holy Spirit comes on you; and you will be my witnesses in Jerusalem, and in all Judea and Samaria, and to the ends of the earth" (Acts 1:8). He told them that a life-changing encounter with the Holy Spirit would result in a world-changing ministry.

In Jesus' earthly ministry, He lived as a human being—within time and physical space as we know them. He chose to place those limitations on Himself when He left heaven and was born as a baby in Bethlehem. He became a man so He could be our Savior (Phil. 2:5–8). During His earthly lifetime, He could be in only one place at a time. After He returned to heaven, Jesus sent His Spirit to guide and equip His followers. Through the Spirit, Christ can be everywhere with everyone at once—omnipresent, an attribute of God.

Following Jesus' resurrection and ascension into heaven, the Holy Spirit arrived while the disciples were gathered to fellowship and celebrate together during a religious festival in Jerusalem:

"When the day of Pentecost came, they were all together in one place. Suddenly a sound like the blowing of a violent wind came from heaven and filled the whole house where they were sitting. They saw what seemed to be tongues of fire that separated and came to rest on each of them. All of them were filled with the Holy Spirit and began to speak in other tongues as the Spirit enabled them" (Acts 2:1–4).

Notice that the Holy Spirit filled them, and He enabled them. They were given a dynamic ability to preach and teach the message of salvation in the native languages of the thousands who had gathered in Jerusalem that day. That was a direct fulfillment of Jesus' twin prophecy, "You will receive power," and "You will be My witnesses" (Acts 1:8).

Where is the Holy Spirit now? He's in the hearts and lives of His people, enabling them to live pure, powerful, and productive lives. When by faith you confess Jesus Christ as your Savior and Lord—accepting His payment for your sin and asking Him to forgive you and receive you into His family—He comes to live within you: "Because you are sons, God sent the Spirit of His Son into our hearts" (Gal. 4:6).

As we have seen before, as followers of the Lord Jesus Christ, we are dwelling places of God. His Spirit lives within us: "In Him you too are being built together to become a dwelling in which God lives by His Spirit" (Eph. 2:22). What an incredible reality!

3. Why Is the Holy Spirit Living in You?

We've established who the Holy Spirit is—God. And we've seen where He resides—in the life of a follower of Christ. Now, let's look at the reason why the Holy Spirit is made available to the believer. In the process, we will discover how important it is to let Him have complete control of our lives.

Even though the Holy Spirit comes to reside in us when we receive Jesus Christ, He may not be in control. He may be living there as an honored guest. We may acknowledge His presence, but we make sure He doesn't interfere with our attitudes or actions—just what we would expect of a guest in our home. This attitude of self-control is part of the natural rebellion against God that we inherited from Adam and Eve: "The sinful nature desires what is contrary to the Spirit, and the Spirit what is contrary to the sinful nature. They are in conflict with each other, so that you do not do what you want" (Gal. 5:17).

We have also seen that living under the control of self results in spiritual disorder and defeat. That is why we are commanded through the apostle Paul to "be filled with the Holy Spirit." By advising us to be under the influence/control of the Holy Spirit, he tells us to settle the control controversy, and to experience the joy, peace, and spiritual power in giving our futile efforts at control to God. (See the contrast between self-control and Spirit-control in Gal. 5:19–25.)

A friend shared this helpful illustration with me several years ago. Imagine that I come to your house and knock on your front door. You open the door and invite me in. Then you take me to a tiny spare room and escort me inside. You then turn to leave and lock the door behind you. Am I in your house? Yes, of course. But I am confined to the spare room. Sometimes we're tempted to put Jesus conveniently in the "spare room."

We often divide our lives into compartments. We have the Sunday compartment, the home compartment, the work compartment, the pleasure compartment, and so on. Do you get the picture? It comes down to a control issue. Who will control your life—you or the Lord? The God of the universe did not come into your life to be locked in a spare room. If you are to enjoy and fully benefit from this living relationship with the Holy Spirit, He needs to have full control of every room in your life.

THE ADVANTAGES OF BEING FILLED WITH THE HOLY SPIRIT

In his prayer for Christians at Ephesus, Paul revealed what the Holy Spirit will do for you after you ask Him to take control of your life:

> I pray that out of His glorious riches He may strengthen you with power through His Spirit in your inner being, so that Christ may dwell in your hearts through faith. And I pray that you, being rooted and established in love, may have power, together with all the saints, to grasp how wide and long and high and deep is the love of Christ, and to know this love that surpasses knowledge—that you may be filled to the measure of all the fullness of God. Now to Him who is able to do immeasurably more than all we ask or imagine, according to His power that is at work within us, (Eph. 3:16–20)

In Paul's prayer, notice seven specific advantages of living a Spirit-filled life:

1. Spiritual strength: "Strengthen you with power through His Spirit in your inner being"

2. Victorious faith: "So that Christ may dwell in your hearts through faith"

3. Power to love others: "Being rooted and established in love, may have power"

4. Spiritual belonging: "Grasp how wide and long and high and deep is the love of Christ, and to know this love that surpasses knowledge"

5. Christlikeness: "That you may be filled to the measure of all the fullness of God"

6. Power in prayer: "To Him who is able to do immeasurably more than all we ask or imagine"

7. Power for living: "According to His power that is at work within us"

There are many other advantages, including peace and harmony with others: "Make every effort to keep the unity of the Spirit through the bond of peace" (Eph. 4:3). The Spirit-filled life provides motivation for all kinds of Christlike behavior: "For the fruit of the light consists in all goodness, righteousness and truth" (Eph. 5:9).

HOW TO BE FILLED WITH THE HOLY SPIRIT

Though we experience the filling of the Holy Spirit uniquely, God has given us common criteria in His Word.

1. Be Certain That You Have Been Born Again

Remember the verse mentioned earlier in the chapter: "Because you are sons, God sent the Spirit of His Son into our hearts" (Gal. 4:6). The Spirit-filled life is for sons, those who have accepted God's invitation and become His children through Jesus' sacrifice. The Holy Spirit is given to all Christians to accompany, lead, and equip us in evangelizing the world. It is imperative that you have the assurance that you have first given your heart's allegiance to Christ and have the assurance of His forgiveness and acceptance.

2. Walk in Obedient Fellowship with the Lord

Jesus said, "If you love Me, you will obey what I command. And I will ask the Father, and He will give you another Counselor to be with you forever—the Spirit of truth" (John 14:15–17). Be open to obey God's unfolding plan for your spiritual life. Obedience also includes confessing every known sin to God. The promised Holy Spirit was given to followers of Jesus Christ who waited in faithful obedience. An attitude of obedience to all that God *asks* leads to receiving all that God *gives*.

3. Surrender Everything You Know of Yourself to Everything You Know of God

Paul wrote, "I urge you, brothers, in view of God's mercy, to offer your bodies as living sacrifices, holy and pleasing to God— this is your spiritual act of worship" (Rom. 12:1). To be filled with the Holy Spirit is to be under His control; that control includes every area of your life. You are making Him the Lord of your life. You are deciding that He will no longer be an honored guest in your heart and life. Rather, He will be the Master of the house.

4. Stand on the Authority of God's Word

God has given us promises upon which we can take a spiritual stand: "This is the confidence we have in approaching God: that if we ask anything according to His will, He hears us. And if we know that He hears us—whatever we ask—we know that we have what we asked of Him" (1 John 5:14–15).

When it comes to the Spirit-filled life, God's command is

very plain: "Be filled with the Holy Spirit." If He commanded you to be filled, surely it is His will for you. And He promised to both hear your request and fulfill it.

5. Ask in Faith

In his gospel, Luke gave us a beautiful picture of a natural father's intent to provide the best for his children. It's a warm example of the heavenly Father's commitment to supply the spiritual needs of His own: "If you then, though you are evil, know how to give good gifts to your children, how much more will your Father in heaven give the Holy Spirit to those who ask Him!" (Luke 11:13). In other words, if you have known earthly parents (in their natural state of evil) who are willing to give gifts solely for your benefit, then the heavenly Father's loving intent is infinitely greater.

The bottom line: ask for the filling of God's Spirit in confidence. How did you receive Christ as your Lord and Savior? By faith! So it is by faith that you are filled with the Holy Spirit. You do not need to beg God for this experience. He longs for you to experience His presence through the power of the Holy Spirit as a way of life. The Spirit-filled life is the normal Christian life!

SUMMARY TRUTHS ABOUT THE HOLY SPIRIT

There is no final word—apart from God's—on the subject of the Spirit-filled life. This vital Christian experience may be called by different names, interpreted by various nuances and teachings, and encountered uniquely by unique personalities. However, the summary truths lead us to some basic facts:

- God is not the author of confusion. He wants you to be clear about being filled with His Spirit. God will never command you to experience something and then make it difficult for you to obtain that experience.

- God loves you supremely and wants the very best for your spiritual life.

- God wants to have a dynamic and growing relationship with you—a relationship that is enhanced by totally surrendering to His loving will.

- God has made the ultimate sacrifice—the offering of His only Son—so that you may enjoy spiritual power over the enemy of your soul and the attitude of the world.

Jesus modeled a victorious life. He gave Himself to provide for your victory, returned to heaven in victory, and sent the Holy Spirit to live in you to assure your Source of victory.

10

SPIRITUAL BREATHING

Since our two children have graduated from high school and moved on to college and work, Barbara and I have had time to catch up on some projects around our house. For the first time, we worked with a professional landscaper to choose shrubs and greenery for the entranceway to our house. When my son was home on break, he helped me dig out the old shrubs and we all worked to plant the bushes and flowers recommended by the landscaper. When our project was finally finished, it looked great! The plants were healthy and green; the mulch was fresh and dark. It even smelled good.

But after the honeymoon period, our great landscaping job required a lot of work. Weeds popped up, the new bushes needed water and the mulch had to be raked over to look fresh again. We're still proud of our work and happy to have attractive greenery in front of our house, but we can't just sit back and admire the beauty. There's always another job to be done.

When you make a lifelong commitment to God, He revolutionizes your world. You begin your Christian life with a great sense of relief and freedom. You have been delivered from the bondage of your past. You are part of a great new spiritual family. You have a future as bright as the promises of God. But what happens when the spiritual newness wears off? What if you find yourself reverting to your old ways? Can a Christian sin? Yes. Does a Christian have to live in fear of sinning? No. "For you did not receive a spirit that makes you a slave again to fear, but you received the Spirit of sonship. And by Him we cry, 'Abba, Father'" (Rom. 8:15).

The Bible warns us about backpedaling in our spiritual lives. In the New Testament, the entire book of Hebrews was written to Christians who were reverting to their old ways: "See to it, brothers, that none of you has a sinful, unbelieving heart that turns away from the living God. But encourage one another daily, as long as it is called Today, so that none of you may be hardened by sin's deceitfulness. We have come to share in Christ if we hold firmly till the end the confidence we had at first" (Heb. 3:12–14).

Often the letters of the apostles to the local churches cautioned Christians about spiritual neglect. The apostle Paul gave this stern reminder to the church in Galatia: "You are no longer a slave, but a son; and since you are a son, God has made you also an heir. Formerly, when you did not know God, you were slaves to those who by nature are not gods. But now that you know God—or rather are known by God—how is it that you are turning back to those weak and miserable principles? Do you wish to be enslaved by them all over again?" (Gal. 4:7–9).

Paul also challenged one of his star pupils, a young pastor in the first-century church named Timothy, about staying fresh in his faith:

> Don't let anyone look down on you because you are young, but set an example for the believers in speech, in life, in love, in faith and in purity. Until I come, devote yourself to the public reading of Scripture, to preaching and to teaching. Do

not neglect your gift, which was given you through a
prophetic message when the body of elders laid their hands on
you. Be diligent in these matters; give yourself wholly to them,
so that everyone may see your progress. Watch your life and
doctrine closely. Persevere in them, because if you do, you will
save both yourself and your hearers. (1 Tim. 4:12–16)

PROCEED WITH CAUTION

A few weeks after starting a stained glass class in high school, my
daughter brought a project home. She understood the concepts
and had practiced some of the techniques of stained glass art. She
worked carefully to scratch and break each piece of glass according to a pattern she designed. But when she cut her finger
smoothing foil along an edge of glass, she truly learned to proceed with caution.

As a new Christian, you're not sealed away into a monastery
or convent to avoid worldly temptations. You have the instructions (God's Word), and I pray that you find a mature Christian
to teach and mentor you. When you are looking for a mentor,
find an older person of your gender at your church whom you
enjoy and whose godly lifestyle you admire. (You may want to
ask your pastor to recommend an experienced Christian who
would be a wise teacher and encourager for you. After praying
about your choice, ask the person whether he or she would consider being your mentor.) But even with the most godly and
helpful training you will inevitably encounter pitfalls and temptations. We do not live our Christian lives in morbid fear of sinning against God's will. Yet we should be cautious about the
attitudes and actions that put us in conflict with His will. What
happens when you, as a Christian, sin? John the apostle wrote,

> If we claim to have fellowship with Him yet walk in the darkness, we lie and do not live by the truth. But if we walk in the light, as He is in the light, we have fellowship with one another, and the blood of Jesus, His Son, purifies us from all sin. If we claim to be without sin, we deceive ourselves and the truth is not in us. If we confess our sins, He is faithful and just and will forgive us our sins and purify us from all unrighteousness. (1 John 1:6–9)

Just as God has made a way to deliver us from bondage to our past, He has made a provision for our future deliverance. Though we are not free from the *possibility* of sin, we certainly don't have to live in bondage to sin. The provision that Jesus Christ made available by shedding His blood on the cross is continually available to us for living a victorious Christian life.

You don't have to spend one minute disconnected from God. It's as simple as taking your next breath. What do I mean? Spiritual breathing is a spiritual exercise that you can do to maintain a vital relationship with God. Many people who have trusted Christ as their Savior are still living on the equivalent of a spiritual rollercoaster. They go from one emotional experience to another. If they are honest with themselves, they will admit they are living with spiritual frustration and defeat. If that's how you feel, spiritual breathing will enable you to escape the emotional ride and experience victory in your Christian life. God really does want you to live the adventure to the full. Jesus declared, "I have come that they may have life, and have it to the full" (John 10:10).

"What if I don't feel like a Christian?" you may ask. Sometimes you will not feel very holy. You will have spiritual doubts. You may feel that everything is crumbling around you. Your Christian mentors and heroes will let you down. Remember that Satan causes you to doubt God's promises. He is the enemy of your soul, and he especially uses emotional feelings to distract you from faith.

Remember, we do *not* rely on our feelings. We have the potential to experience every emotion that is common to humanity. But there are at least two things you should always remember.

1. We Are Not Saved by Our Feelings!

My salvation is not controlled by my feelings. Feelings are fickle. Feelings change, based on the circumstances of life. Salvation is based on what God has done for me and in me. I put my faith in Christ alone.

2. God's Love for Us Never Fails

Regardless of how I feel, I have these promises from God:

God has said,
"Never will I leave you;
    never will I forsake you."
So we say with confidence,
    "The Lord is my helper; I will not be afraid.
    What can man do to me?" (Heb. 13:5–6)

The LORD is my shepherd, I shall not be in want.
    He makes me lie down in green pastures,
He leads me beside quiet waters,
    He restores my soul.
He guides me in paths of righteousness
    for His name's sake.
Even though I walk
    through the valley of the shadow of death,

I will fear no evil,
>   for You are with me;
Your rod and Your staff,
>   they comfort me.
You prepare a table before me
>   in the presence of my enemies.
You anoint my head with oil;
>   my cup overflows.
Surely goodness and love will follow me
>   all the days of my life,
and I will dwell in the house of the LORD forever. (Ps. 23)

Fluctuations in your spiritual feelings are perfectly normal. Many factors affect your emotions—the weather forecast, your physical health, or the latest stock market quotes. But your relationship with God is not based on your feelings. Your relationship with God is grounded in faith and the fact that God has done for you exactly what He promised to do. He is faithful. Rely on God, not your feelings.

SIN AND SETBACKS

Christian history—including Bible times—notes those who were once fervent in their faith but suffered spiritual setbacks. A giant of the Old Testament, King David, was called "a man after [God's] own heart" (1 Sam. 13:14). He had an amazing personal relationship with God, but even he succumbed to sin. David earnestly prayed that God would cleanse his heart and "wash away all [his] iniquity" (Ps. 51:2). No matter how holy a life Christians may live, we are not exempt from being tempted to disobey God's law.

One of Christ's disciples, Peter, succumbed to the taunts of Christ's enemies and denied even knowing Him (Matt. 26:69–75). In the New Testament church, a husband and a wife who were members of the new church fell into greed. The early Christians shared everything, even selling pieces of land or houses to provide for the poor among them. But the couple deceitfully kept back a portion of the money they had promised to give:

> Now a man named Ananias, together with his wife Sapphira . . . sold a piece of property. With his wife's full knowledge he kept back part of the money for himself, but brought the rest and put it at the apostles' feet. Then Peter said, "Ananias, how is it that Satan has so filled your heart that you have lied to the Holy Spirit and have kept for yourself some of the money you received for the land?" (Acts 5:1–3)

The book of James, a letter to first-century Christians, instructed the church about dealing with sins. James wrote, "Confess your sins to each other and pray for each other so that you may be healed" (5:16). Far from confessing their dishonesty to the church, Ananias and Sapphira denied Peter's allegation and died.

It deeply saddens my heart when I see another brother or sister in the Lord become involved in sinful behavior. Several years ago, some very visible Christians became involved in sexual sin. Yes, it was a very sad situation, but I must admit that I was a bit smug about the tragedies. I also said I was not surprised. Shortly afterward, a national leader for whom I had great respect became sexually involved with a coworker and was forced to resign his leadership position. His actions affected him, and many people were disappointed and hurt, including me. The situation scared me because I realized that it could happen to anyone.

A few of my minister friends have been forced to leave the ministry because of sin in their lives. Whenever these things happen, I grieve for them. I know it can happen, but it never needs to happen. I encourage you to build hedges of protection around yourself and your relationships. God has promised that "no temptation has seized you except what is common to man. And God is faithful; He will not let you be tempted beyond what you can bear. But when you are tempted, He will also provide a way out so that you can stand up under it" (1 Cor. 10:13).

Of course, you must flee temptation (1 Cor. 6:18). God wants you to live a victorious life. He has provided the way for you to conquer sin. He not only took the first step by sacrificing His own Son on the cross, He also took the next steps—providing the power of His Holy Spirit and the instruction of His Word. When you do sin, God has made a way for you to be restored to a right relationship with Him.

WHAT IS SPIRITUAL BREATHING?

God designed us in such an amazing way! The more I learn about God's creation, the more amazed I become about the universe and the human body, right down to strands of DNA. Some people want us to believe that this all took place by accident. But God spoke this world into existence, and He made you and me and all of creation to live in fellowship with Him. One of the ways that we sustain life is by breathing. We inhale clean air, and our lungs extract oxygen from the air. The oxygen is absorbed into our blood, our lungs exhale the leftover impurities, and life goes on.

What happens if you stop breathing? We both know what will happen. You pass out, and if the problem is not corrected, you die. Breathing is important. It's a vital function of life.

Your spiritual life functions similarly to your physical life. The Bible says, "For the wages of sin is death" (Rom. 6:23). If the impurities that you inhale physically are not exhaled, you die. If sin remains in your life and is not exhaled, it can lead to physical and spiritual death. The difference is that spiritual death is eternal!

If you had a severe breathing problem and I had a solution, you would expect me to help. In fact, I believe you would do exactly what I told you to do because your life depended on my solution.

If there is sin in your life and you have not confessed it, your problem is even more serious. I suggest you follow these instructions because your spiritual life depends on it. By the way, these are not my instructions—they are God's, clearly explained in His Word.

EXHALE

Like the physical breathing maintaining your body, spiritual breathing maintains and invigorates your spiritual self. The first step in the spiritual breathing exercise is exhaling. Exhale—confess your sin. We learn in 1 John 1:9 to "confess our sins." *Confess* doesn't mean to tell God or anyone else what sin you committed. You don't have to tell God that you broke one of the Ten Commandments. He already knows. *Confess* means, rather, to agree with God concerning your sin, admitting that what you did was sin. You have probably heard the expression *'fess up*. That means to come clean—to admit it. Confession means to 'fess up. "Yes, Lord, I admit it. I have sinned."

How Will I Know When I Have Sinned Against God?

1. The Holy Spirit convicts us of sin. God has put an internal alarm within you—His Holy Spirit. His indwelt Spirit is faithful to point out the problem areas of your life. Jesus promised that the Holy Spirit would remind you of your sin: "When He comes, He will convict the world of guilt in regard to sin and righteousness and judgment" (John 16:8). The Holy Spirit's convicting is in the form of a gentle (and sometimes not-so-gentle) prodding of your conscience. He makes you uncomfortable over your attitudes or actions that are contrary to His will.

2. God has given us His Word. God's word is written in the Bible, and it is written on our hearts. We are without excuse. We can say, with Adam and Eve, "The devil made me do it!" But the fact is, we choose to sin. In the same way, we must choose to come clean with God and admit what He already knows. The Holy Spirit will often use a scripture verse that you have read or heard to point out the error of your ways. King David reminded us in a psalm,

> The ordinances of the LORD are sure
> > and altogether righteous.
> They are more precious than gold,
> > than much pure gold;
> they are sweeter than honey,
> > than honey from the comb.
> By them is your servant warned;
> > in keeping them there is great reward. (Ps. 19:9–11)

Once you are aware of an attitude or action that is contrary to the known will of God, immediately confess it to Him. His voice is not loud and condemning; rather, it is still and assuring. The psalmist King David had experienced not only God's great blessings but also severe punishments for his sins. Yet he wrote that even God's rules are "sweeter than honey." Don't be alarmed when the Lord corrects you. There is a positive perspective to that correction. It is an indication of your genuine faith and connection to God. The Bible says,

> Do not make light of the Lord's discipline,
>> and do not lose heart when He rebukes you,
> because the Lord disciplines those He loves. (Heb. 12:5–6)

INHALING

The next step in spiritual breathing is to inhale. Inhaling is receiving God's forgiveness. God has promised in His Word, "If we confess our sins, He is faithful and just and will forgive us our sins" (1 John 1:9). Spiritually breathe in the life-giving "oxygen" of His forgiveness. Pray, "Thank You, God, for forgiving me according to the promise of Your Word." Your act of thanksgiving is a step of faith, believing with all your heart that God has done what He promised to do. Remember, "faith is being sure of what we hope for" (Heb. 11:1).

As you inhale, you ask God to fill you anew with His Holy Spirit. You may be thinking, *You already talked about the Spirit-filled life in the last chapter!* Yes, that is the normal Christian life, but it is not a once-in-a-lifetime event. If you are to be filled with the Holy Spirit as a way of life, you must keep your account with the Lord current.

We learn from God's Word that we are to say yes to the things that please God and no to the things that displease Him. When you sin, you make the heart of God sad, and the Holy

Spirit living in you is grieved. At that point you are no longer under the Spirit's guidance. When you sin, you take back the controls from the Holy Spirit. The only way to restore Him to His rightful place on the throne of your heart is to exhale (confess) and inhale (receive a fresh filling of the Holy Spirit). You then come back under the Spirit's control.

Someone asked the great Chicago preacher D. L. Moody, "Why do you always pray to be filled with the Holy Spirit? Don't you believe God has already done that?" He replied, "Yes, I know God has filled me, but I leak." We all leak, and we all need to learn the concept of spiritual breathing.

I have met many Christians who can look back at the moment and place they said yes to Jesus. They prayed and asked Jesus to forgive them, but for whatever reason they have not maintained a fresh account with the Lord. Rather than experiencing spiritual victory, they live with discouragement and spiritual defeat. The enemy has them in bondage because of the sin in their lives.

Years ago, I attended a retreat sponsored by the youth ministry Campus Crusade for Christ. Dr. Bill Bright shared with us the concept of spiritual breathing. He then asked us to do something that I found to be encouraging. He asked us to take a notebook and get alone with the Lord. I found a spot outside under a tree. I wrote down every sin I could remember committing. (Dr. Bright gave us the entire afternoon to work on this project.) You may think that would be depressing, but it was one of the most freeing experiences of my Christian life. I still remember the release I felt when I was finished. When I could not think of anything else to write, I prayed, "Lord if there is anything else that I need to confess, please help me to remember." I turned to 1 John 1:9 and read, "If we confess our sin, He is faithful and just and will forgive us our sins and purify us from all unrighteousness."

I then wrote 1 John 1:9 all over my list. I took the list out of the notebook and tore it to shreds. I took it back to my room and got some matches and burned it in the trash can. After destroying the list, I turned to Psalm 103:12 and read, "As far as the east is from the west, so far has He removed our transgressions from us." In Hebrews 8:12, I read, "For I will forgive their wickedness and will remember their sins no more." What promises! I encourage you to get alone with God. Take only your Bible, a pen, and some paper. Make your list and then destroy it. The list is between you and God. If the Lord reminds you that you need to make restoration for a sinful act, do it. If He reminds you to work at restoring a broken relationship do it.

I can say with full reverence for God that you and I can remember things today that God has chosen to no longer remember. I can still remember my past sins, but God has chosen to forget them. If God has chosen to forgive and forget, we should not live in bondage to the past! If you have put your faith in Christ alone, you are forgiven. You are free. Live in victory.

SPIRITUAL EXERCISE

As I have already said, you don't have to live with the probability of sin hanging over your Christian life. You can have spiritual victory through the power of Christ. But you are well advised to be on the alert—protecting your heart and mind from the things that will draw your spiritual attention from God: "Above all else, guard your heart, for it is the wellspring of life" (Prov. 4:23). A key area of temptation for our culture includes the media—television, video, movies, and the Internet. Put a guard around what you watch and what you hear.

Olympic athletes do not live in fear of becoming morbidly

obese. They have already developed a rigorous routine of workouts and strict nutrition. These athletes focus on maintaining their daily commitments. As a child of God, you must focus on your daily spiritual exercise. The most important and effective way to guard against sin is to keep the communication lines open between you and God. Pray daily. Read the Bible. If Satan can hinder you from communicating with God—perhaps skipping your morning quiet time—he has begun to accomplish his evil purpose.

Just as physical exercise strengthens your body, spiritual exercise strengthens your soul. There are some spiritual disciplines that will strengthen your inner spirit, including worshiping, serving, giving, witnessing to your faith, and having fellowship with other Christians. If you have a daily workout at the gym or a weekly jogging schedule, you know the dedication required for those routines, especially at the beginning. But you also have experienced the great feeling of accomplishment and health after your workout. Be intentional about planning your spiritual exercise and follow through to reap the benefits and blessings.

THE LONG-TERM BENEFITS
OF SPIRITUAL BREATHING

Spiritual breathing will heighten your spiritual sensitivity and will cause you to focus your attention on God. God wants you to have a vibrant, life-changing relationship with Him. In Revelation 3, the apostle John wrote to a church in the city of Laodicea. The people were once active for God, but their faith had mellowed into lethargy. The Lord told them, "I know your deeds, that you are neither cold nor hot. I wish you were either one or the other! So, because you are lukewarm—neither hot nor cold—I am about to spit you out of my mouth" (Rev. 3:15).

Halfhearted Christianity is detestable to God because He knows how it rots the very core of our souls. He wants more for us. Spiritual breathing gives us constant fellowship with God. Serving Christ is not just about a one-time act of commitment to Christ. It is a continual, life-changing, daily relationship with the victorious living Savior of the world. Practice spiritual breathing as a way of life, and you will never again need to make another list of old sins!

11

WHAT IS YOUR RELATIONSHIP
TO HIS CHURCH?

What comes to mind when you hear the word *church*? A building? Perhaps you describe the church as a group of people getting together to learn about God. Worship celebrations? An organization? Actually the church of Jesus Christ is more than all of that. The church is people. It is a dynamic organism that is figuratively living and growing. Jesus described the church as His body.

A number of years ago, I was the pastor of a church in Roanoke, Virginia. One morning, I stopped at the local donut shop for a cup of coffee and—to be completely honest—a donut too. I sat at the counter, and after I was served, I began a casual conversation with the person sitting next to me. He soon asked me, "What do you do for a living?" I said, "I am a pastor." "Where is your church?" he asked. I decided to have some fun with my new friend and responded to his question with, "I don't know." He looked confused. Thinking I misunderstood his question, he again asked, "Where is your church?" I responded with even greater emphasis, "I don't know!" I could tell from the look on his face that he thought I was not playing with a full deck.

"Let me get this straight. You are a pastor, and you don't know where your church meets?"

"Oh, you mean where we meet!" I said. "Well, on Sunday morning we meet at 3600 Peter's Creek Road. Since this is Monday morning, the church I pastor is scattered all over the city and beyond. Some people are at their offices in Roanoke and the surrounding area, some are at home, others are at school, and at least one is in Chicago for the week." My new friend got the point, and we had a great conversation that morning about church.

Paul described it this way: "The body is a unit, though it is made up of many parts; and though all its parts are many, they form one body. So it is with Christ. For we were all baptized by one Spirit into one body—whether Jews or Greeks, slave or free—and we were all given the one Spirit to drink" (1 Cor. 12:12–13).

The word *baptized* means "to be placed into"—placed into one body. As we have already seen, everyone who is reconciled to God through faith in the Lord Jesus Christ becomes part of an unseen organization: the family of God, the church. John explained, "To all who received Him, to those who believed in His name, He gave the right to become children of God—children born not of natural descent, nor of human decision or a husband's will, but born of God" (John 1:12–13).

The church is one of the most enduring and influential institutions known to humankind. Jesus promised, "I will build my church, and the gates of Hades will not overcome it" (Matt. 16:18). In other words, "I will establish a church that even the forces of hell will not be able to eliminate."

History proves the truth of Christ's promise. Followers of Jesus Christ have been misunderstood, maligned, ignored, and disregarded. They have been beaten publicly and imprisoned privately. Yet their numbers are in the billions, and they continue to increase daily. Even in the most oppressive societies, the church is growing in unprecedented numbers. While other institutions fall during bad times, the church thrives. It valiantly and victoriously marches on, undimmed by the attitudes and actions of its critics. It is doubtless the greatest institution that you will ever become a part of.

As you've already seen, the Romanian church has greatly impacted my life. I am indebted to the body of Christ in Romania and many friends whom God has used to teach and shape me. Under communism, the Romanian church and her leaders were brutally persecuted. Romania's iron-fisted Communist dictator, Nicolae Ceausescu, intended to destroy the Romanian church.

Shortly after the fall of communism in Romania, Ceausescu was executed for crimes and atrocities committed against Romania and her people. Almost twenty-five years before his execution, Ceausescu said, "In thirty years, there will be no church in Romania. Communism will have created such a utopia, there will be no need for the church."

A visit to Romania makes clear the devastating effects of communism. It is impossible to fully explain how the Communist system victimized the nation and her people. When former President Ronald Reagan referred to communism as an "evil empire," he was 100 percent correct. Today, the system that tried to destroy the church has fallen, and the church survives!

The Romanian church stands as a living testimony to the power of God. Far from being eliminated, the Romanian church is alive and growing, while communism has been destroyed. Romania has the largest Pentecostal church in all of Europe.

Romania is also home to Europe's largest baptist church. I have had the great joy and honor to preach in both churches.

THE FIRST-CENTURY CHURCH: A MODEL CHURCH

Jesus' prophecy regarding the church is best seen in the light of the first-century church. The New Testament book of Acts, named for the Acts of the Apostles, is perhaps the most complete resource for understanding the concept of the church. It is a historical account of the first Christians during the time that followed Christ's ascension into the heavens. It describes the character and early organization of what we know as the church. It is also a detailed and appealing picture of what Christ intended His followers to experience. The early church experienced phenomenal growth. And the church remains alive and well more than two thousand years later.

The first-century believers in the Lord Jesus Christ didn't meet in a church building, as we often do today. The early church met either in the Jewish temple courts or in the homes of individuals: "Every day they continued to meet together in the temple courts. They broke bread in their homes and ate together with glad and sincere hearts" (Acts 2:46). The main focus of the church was people meeting together in the name of the Lord Jesus Christ for instruction, encouragement, and fellowship. The church is God's instrument for reaching the world.

Basically the agenda has not changed. Because of the variety of people across the world that make up local churches, the church varies in administration and organization, interpretations of beliefs, and styles of worship. Yet its original purpose is intact: to tell the world about salvation through Christ.

THE IMPORTANCE OF THE CHURCH

Today it is equally—if not more—important for followers of Jesus Christ to meet together for the same reasons that the early church met. The New Testament writer gave excellent advice: "Let us not give up meeting together, as some are in the habit of doing, but let us encourage one another—and all the more as you see the Day approaching" (Heb. 10:25). The "Day" is the return of the Lord Jesus Christ to the earth. The Bible says that a day is coming when Jesus will come for His followers to take us to an eternal dwelling place that He has prepared for us (John 14:1–2).

Once you have decided to follow Jesus Christ, your entire worldview is completely changed. You will naturally want to be around others who have made the same decision. That fellowship of believers—the church—serves as an incubator for the development of your Christian faith. Participation in a local church is not essential for salvation, but it is essential for spiritual growth. A newborn baby needs gentle, loving care to grow and develop into an adult. In the same way, "newborn" Christians need to be nurtured in their walk with the Lord by other mature Christians. Let me offer several reasons why you should be involved in a local fellowship of believers.

1. God Communicates Through the Church

Christians commonly believe that the church was born on the Jewish festival day of Pentecost following Jesus Christ's crucifixion and resurrection. Earlier, we learned about God sending the Holy Spirit on that same day (see Chapter 9). God communicated the birth of the church by sending an unusual sign: "When the day of Pentecost came, they were all together in one place. Suddenly a sound like the blowing of a violent wind came from heaven and filled the whole house where they were sitting. They saw what seemed to be tongues of fire that separated and came to rest on each of them" (Acts 2:1–3).

This unusual communication from heaven signaled a new era for the followers of Christ. It is significant that the believers were "together in one place" when they received it. God could have communicated the truth of this great event to an individual, just as He communicated the coming of the Messiah Savior, Jesus Christ, to Mary and to Joseph. Instead, He chose to communicate the marvelous message to a group of believers, ushering in the church age.

God still uses the local church to communicate His Word and His will to believers. The first-century church had a regularly scheduled time of worship and instruction: the first day of the week. It may have been chosen to celebrate the resurrection of the Lord Jesus Christ (Matt. 28:1–7). The apostle Paul gave instructions for the collection and distribution of church funds to believers meeting on their regular worship day, "on the first day of every week" (1 Cor. 16:2).

Each time Christians gather together for worship and instruction, God uses the occasion to communicate His truth. Bible readings, teaching and preaching, singing, praying encouragement and advice of other Christians are what the church is about. Each facet of group worship is a way for God, through His Spirit, to communicate instruction, assurance, warning, and motivation to His people. I urge you to become a part of a local church where God communicates His truth. You need the church, and the church needs you. The church is God's organization. Failing to be involved in the life of the church is direct disobedience of the Word of God.

2. Spiritual Gifts and Abilities

The history of the church, as recorded in the Acts of the Apostles, also chronicles the individual ministries of believers. God the Holy Spirit has given a unique ability to every person. These abilities are to be used in the development of the church for the glory of God. Your gift is energized and given a focus at the time of your conversion. The Bible teaches us about these spiritual gifts: "There are different kinds of gifts, but the same Spirit. There are different kinds of service, but the same Lord. There are different kinds of working, but the same God works all of them in all men. Now to each one the manifestation of the Spirit is given for the common good" (1 Cor. 12:4–7).

According to the Bible, some of the gifts/abilities include the following:

- Teaching

- Preaching

- Serving

- Giving

- Hospitality

- Evangelism

The Holy Spirit gives believers these abilities for a specific purpose: "So that the body of Christ may be built up until we all reach unity in the faith and in the knowledge of the Son of God and become mature, attaining to the whole measure of the fullness of Christ" (Eph. 4:12–13).

The church offers a place to develop the abilities that God has given you. You see, God has graciously endowed you with the ability to make a unique contribution to a local church. Participating in a local fellowship of believers gives you the satisfaction of serving in a fulfilling ministry. You also benefit from the unique gifts of other believers. God wants to use His church to shape you into the person He wants you to be and to use your gifts to build His church.

3. The Church Is a Place of Learning

You probably have been acquainted with the term *Sunday school* from early childhood. You may have been part of a Sunday school most of your life. And your Sunday school experiences may have run the gamut from terrific to traumatic. But wherever you are on that spectrum, you learned some character lessons in Sunday school that have affected your life in positive ways.

The church is a place for you to gain knowledge—knowledge of Christian character traits that will influence your life and, through you, the lives of many others. The members of the first-century church "devoted themselves to the apostles' teaching" (Acts 2:42). The apostles were the spiritual leaders of the church. They read and explained the Scriptures to their fellow believers. Their collective writings served as a textbook to the new Christians. And their meeting times included long hours of instruction and training for service.

The brand-new message of the church raised many questions among the devout Jewish people about the new believers. When the signs from heaven announced the coming of the Holy Spirit and the birth of the church on the day of Pentecost, some were "amazed and perplexed, [and] they asked one another, 'What does this mean?'" (Acts 2:12). The apostle Peter took advantage of the teaching moment and delivered one of the great sermons recorded in the Bible. He boldly presented the entire gospel message, quoting the Old Testament prophet Joel to show how the supernatural events fulfilled Joel's prophecy hundreds of years earlier.

He then taught the audience that the death and resurrection of Jesus Christ fulfilled God's plan of reconciliation and forgiveness: "This man [Jesus] was handed over to you by God's set purpose and foreknowledge; and you, with the help of wicked men, put Him to death by nailing Him to the cross. But God raised Him from the dead, freeing Him from the agony of death, because it was impossible for death to keep its hold on Him" (Acts 2:23–24).

God uses the church to bring knowledge to His people. Bible studies, sermons, and age-graded curricula presented through the local church give the believer an overview of God's Word and plan for His creation. Take advantage of the learning opportunities of a local church.

In my life, one of the most significant learning environments of the church has been a small group. Over the past several years they have been more commonly referred to as a cell group. I try to meet with my group once a week. We usually meet for breakfast and then spend time studying and talking about a Scripture passage. We talk about how this particular passage relates to our lives and what we need to do to conform our lives to the Word of God. We pray for each other and hold each other accountable. I encourage you to be involved in a small group as part of your life in church.

4. The Church Fosters Life Change

The church of Jesus Christ is made up of people from all walks of life—the highly educated, the barely educated, the very poor, the wealthy, the old, the young, and many more. Each member of the body of Christ is at a different point in his spiritual journey. Some are making career choices. Others are in the midst of relationship decisions. Some are working through financial strategies. Whatever your immediate need, the church is a place of fellowship and friendship—an ideal place for making life-changing choices.

5. The Church Offers a Support System

The first-century church had a keen sensitivity to the individual needs of its members: "All the believers were together and had everything in common. Selling their possessions and goods, they gave to anyone as he had need. Every day they continued to meet together in the temple courts. They broke bread in their homes and ate together with glad and sincere hearts, praising God and enjoying the favor of all the people" (Acts 2:44–47).

Church gatherings provide social, emotional, and spiritual opportunities for bonding. Church participation will be a vital component of your growth as a young Christian. With mature Christians, you learn by example to walk by faith. Church provides an ideal laboratory for you to see other Christians model a Christ-centered life. You will develop meaningful friendships on deeper levels, and you will experience a sense of belonging.

The church is at its best when it is helping fellow believers during crises. It is beautiful to see a body of believers join together to plan a family dinner for the loved ones of the deceased, provide companionship for homebound people, support hospitalized people, baby-sit the children of a single mom, and do so much more. When people have committed their lives to God and have healthy relationships with one another, God works mightily through them.

This support system is a fulfillment of Jesus' last recorded prayer on the earth. He said, "I pray . . . that all of [the believers] may be one, Father, just as You are in Me and I am in You" (John 17:20–21). The apostle Paul wrote, "There should be no division in the body, but its parts should have equal concern for each other. If one part suffers, every part suffers with it; if one part is honored, every part rejoices with it" (1 Cor. 12:25–26).

The church is a place where you can experience a truly Christian support system. I encourage you to join a church that is alive and well. You can help answer the prayer that Jesus prayed in John 17. What an awesome opportunity we have to be the body of Christ to a world that desperately needs to see love in action!

Dr. John Dresher tells one of my favorite stories. It's about a little girl who is frightened by a violent thunderstorm. She runs to her dad and jumps up to sit on his lap. As any good dad would do, he tries to console her. He says, "Honey, there is no need to be frightened. God loves you!" She looks up at her dad through her tears and says, "Dad, I know God loves me, but right now I need someone to love me with skin on." Well, that's the body of Christ: God's love with skin on! I cannot think of a better definition of the church.

We have a wonderful opportunity to show a sin-sick world what life can be like when Jesus is allowed to be Lord of our lives. A sad fact is that the church, Christ's body, is often divided. Far too often we have acted as though the group that meets down the road or across town from our church building is an enemy. But no Christian group is the enemy. Satan and his demons are the enemies of your soul and the church. All parts of the body of Christ may not look alike or act alike, but we should never fight with another member of the body.

CHOOSING YOUR CHURCH

Every church is different, and not all churches will suit your particular tastes or meet your particular needs. Churches have personalities and characteristics just like people do. Some churches are noisy and growing. Others are quiet and maintaining. Which is best? The question really should be: "Which is best for you?" There are many factors to consider in choosing a local church for worship, instruction, service, and fellowship.

1. Pray About Your Search

Above all, you need the Lord's direction in finding a church home. The Bible says, "In his heart a man plans his course, but the LORD determines his steps" (Prov. 16:9). Ask God to direct your plans.

2. Be Certain That It Teaches the Bible As God's Word

A church that doesn't consider the Bible to be the inspired Word of God will not be suitable for your Christian growth. Ask the pastor or a church representative what that church teaches about the Bible. If the Bible is not considered to be absolutely true, then all of the teachings of that church are not fundamentally sound.

3. Ask About Its Beliefs on the Fundamental Teaching of the Bible

What are the core beliefs of the church? Ask the pastor or a representative of the church what the church believes about several basic biblical truths.

Creation. Who created the universe? Is God recognized as its Creator, or does the church subscribe to a more humanistic philosophy about origins?

Human nature. What does the church believe about humankind's basic condition? Does it acknowledge that we are born with a tendency to disobey God (sin), or does it believe that we are basically good and can work our way to heaven by good deeds?

Salvation. What about deliverance from our basic sinfulness? What does the church believe is the way of salvation? Is Christ the only Savior? Is there a way to be forgiven of sin and given a hope for the future other than Christ?

God. What does the church believe about God? Does it believe in the Trinity—that God is three persons in one: Father, Son, and Holy Spirit? Does it say Jesus Christ is the only Son of God? Does the church teach that the Holy Spirit is an actual person?

Life after death. What does the church believe about heaven and hell? Does it acknowledge that God has prepared an eternal home in heaven for those who have professed faith in the Lord Jesus Christ? Does it teach that God has also reserved a place of eternal torment for those who make the choice to reject His mercy?

4. Inquire About the Church's Ministries

Attending or joining a church that has effective ministries to individuals or families is essential to spiritual growth. As you would ask a friend to recommend a business, a doctor, or a school, talk to someone from the church you are considering. Ask about its basic ministries.

What is its style of worship? Some churches have upbeat worship with hand clapping, a praise band, and choruses in an informal atmosphere. Other churches have a more sedate and formal worship style. Some have robed choirs, sing traditional hymns, and read responsive prayers. Where will you be able to focus on worshiping the Lord?

Is it a friendly church? Does it freely welcome new attendees? How does it incorporate newcomers into its mainstream? Some churches are "run" by only a few families.

How does the church promote spiritual growth? Does it have age-graded curricula for children? Are there small groups that are easy to join? What are the opportunities for learning about the Bible?

What about the church's fellowship activities? Are there opportunities for bonding with other believers? Is there a support system for singles? Does it offer activities geared to families? Is there a children's ministry? What about the youth program?

What is the church's vision for outreach? Does it have a plan for supporting missions? Does it seek to lead other people to Christ? Are there opportunities to use your spiritual gifts/abilities to enlarge God's kingdom on earth? Would you feel comfortable bringing your non-Christian friends with you?

What is the church's plan for the future? Does it have a long-range plan for expanding its ministries in the community? Are the worship and educational facilities adequate? If not, are there plans for building or renovation? A church without a vision is not a growing church.

5. Consider Its Demographics

You may want to ask the pastor or a representative of the church about the people of the church.

What is the average age of the church constituency? Is it full of baby boomers? Is it composed mostly of retirees? Are there young adults, teenagers, and singles? How many young families are involved?

What is the pastoral staff ratio to the congregation? Does one person pastor the church or are there assistant pastors as well?

Does it have full-time youth pastor, children's ministry, and music director? How does the pastoral staff minister directly to the congregation?

This is certainly not an inclusive list, but I hope you find it helpful when you choose a local congregation. More than anything, seek wisdom from the Holy Spirit. As you pray about choosing a church, He will give you guidance.

6. Serve As a Member of the Body

Ask yourself, *Is this the place that God has directed me to serve Him as a member of His body?* Yes, the body of Christ, His church, is to be a place where you are encouraged and where you grow spiritually. But just as each part of your physical body has a function, you as a part of His body have a purpose: you are to serve. You do not join the body just to go along for the ride. There is work to be done. God did not give you the institution of the church so that you would have more activities to add to your calendar. Organized worship in the church is a place where you can honor God and enrich your life and the lives of those you love.

HOW DID THEY GROW?

When I was attending Eastern Mennonite College, President Myron Augsburger said, "The reason the early church grew was because it outthought, outlived, and out-died everyone around it." I firmly agree.

The early church grew in a phenomenal way. It began with three thousand people on the day of Pentecost. A few days later, there were five thousand members. Soon there were ten thousand. They finally stopped counting and referred to the number of people as a "multitude." In Acts 5, Jerusalem's high priest grew jealous of the growing church. He forbade the apostles to keep preaching. When they continued, he was furious. He told the new believers, "You have filled Jerusalem with your teaching" (v. 28). Later in the book of Acts it is said of the New Testament church, "These who have turned the world upside down have come here too" (Acts 17:6 NKJV). May it be said of you and me and the entire body of Christ, "You have filled (*the name of your city*) with your teaching! These people who have turned the world upside down have come here too!"

How did the people in the New Testament church do it?

They Outthought

Does that mean they were smarter than anyone else of their day? Well, it takes only a short reading of the Gospels and the book of Acts to realize that most of the early disciples were uneducated. They might have been smart, but they certainly were not the most educated people of their society.

If it is true that the members of the early church outthought the religious leaders of their day, how did they do it? We can learn their methods and how to apply them to our lives:

1. "But God chose the foolish things of the world to shame the wise; God chose the weak things of the world to shame the strong" (1 Cor. 1:27). They recognized their insufficiency as a chance for God to demonstrate His power.

2. "Whenever you are arrested and brought to trial, do not worry beforehand about what to say. Just say whatever is given you at the time, for it is not you speaking, but the Holy Spirit" (Mark 13:11). When they faced persecution and difficulty, they depended on the Holy Spirit to be their Power Source.

3. "When they saw the courage of Peter and John and realized

that they were unschooled, ordinary men, they were astonished and they took note that these men had been with Jesus" (Acts 4:13). We must learn from the early church the importance of spending time with Jesus. Take time to honestly reflect on this question: Do the people around you take note that you have been with Jesus?

They Outlived

What does it mean to outlive others? Does it mean we have a bigger house and more money to spend on "the good life"? Of course not.

Because we are Christians, our quality of life cannot be bought or sold, earned or deserved. This quality of life is not determined by bank accounts or a Who's Who list. And nobody can take it away. It is found only in a living and intimate relationship with the Lord Jesus Christ. It is evidenced in the way we walk and talk. And it improves as we spend time with the Master.

They Out-died

The apostle Paul said, "For to me, to live is Christ and to die is gain" (Phil. 1:21). I suggest that you check out *Martyrs' Mirror* or *Foxe's Book of Martyrs* at your library. Both of these books record the testimonies of men and women who gave their lives for their faith. It has been said, "The church has grown through the blood of her martyrs." I pray that you and I will not be called on to experience this type of death. But whatever our future holds, I know that Christians die well.

Death has been swallowed up in victory.
"Where, O death, is your victory?
Where, O death, is your sting?" (1 Cor. 15:54–55)

12

THERE IS A WAR GOING ON

Yes, there is a war going on! A war that is far more real than Desert Storm, the Vietnam War, the Korean War, World War II, World War I, or any other conflict that has ever raged on planet Earth. The apostle Paul warned Christians to "put on the full armor of God so that you can take your stand against the devil's schemes. For our struggle is not against flesh and blood, but against the rulers, against the authorities, against the powers of this dark world and against the spiritual forces of evil in the heavenly realms" (Eph. 6:11–12).

Many people are totally oblivious to the war. But don't be fooled; it is real! You've seen the devil in cartoons and Halloween costumes. He's portrayed as a feisty-tempered red creature with horns and a pitchfork. Sometimes the devil is pictured as a smirking miniature figure standing on a shoulder, whispering evil thoughts and intentions. Other representations of him are supposed to be scary, humorous, or cute. In reality, he is not cute. He is evil, and he is fighting for your soul and the souls of this generation.

In 1976, Wycliffe Bible Translators invited me to serve as a minister to missionaries in Colombia and Ecuador. I will always remember my first night in the Amazon jungle of Ecuador. We were at the Wycliffe base, not far from where the five missionaries who were trying to take the gospel to the Auca Indians—had been killed by the tribe. Our host built a large fire, and we sat talking around it. I asked my host, "What does it take to become a Wycliffe missionary?" His explanation made a great impact on me, and I have shared his insights with many others.

After meeting all the other qualifications for becoming a Wycliffe missionary, a prospective missionary goes through jungle camp. In jungle camp, you learn what to eat and what not to eat, how to build a house, and basically everything you need to know to survive in the jungle. As a graduation exercise, they drop each participant in the middle of the jungle. If you are still there when the staff returns three days later, you get to be a missionary!

My host explained, "The first thing you do is build a fire." If you ever go to the Amazon jungle, you quickly learn that you do not build a fire to stay warm. The Amazon is extremely hot and humid; the purpose of the fire is to drive away the animals from your camp. The detailed description of his first night in the jungle was amazing. He said, "If you wake up about two in the morning as the fire has died down and you begin to listen, you can hear all kinds of movement in the jungle around your campsite. As the fire grows smaller and smaller, the sounds creep closer and closer into the campsite. As I looked out beyond the circle of light, I could see eyes moving closer." He said, "That gave me a great deal of incentive to get out of my sleeping bag and put more wood on the fire." I thought that if I spent a night in the jungle alone, I would probably stay up all night taking care of the fire!

Does that picture describe your spiritual life? The enemy of your soul is constantly "looking for someone to devour" (1 Peter

5:8). You must stay on guard. Do you need to pile more spiritual wood on the fire of your soul? If the fire that once burned bright in your heart is reduced to a smoldering ember, add some fuel to the coals, and allow the Holy Spirit to fan that glowing ember until your soul once again burns with passion for your Lord.

Before we go any farther, I want to emphatically declare to all who have put their faith in Jesus Christ, "You, dear children, are from God and have overcome them [Satan and his demons], because the One who is in you is greater than the one who is in the world" (1 John 4:4). You do not need to live in fear of the evil one. The devil and all his demons cannot defeat you as long as you keep your eyes and heart set on Jesus. You have acknowledged Him as your Lord and Almighty God; He is more powerful than anything in this physical or spiritual world.

As our Lord returned from forty days of intensive prayer and interaction with His heavenly Father, He taught a valuable lesson:

> Jesus, full of the Holy Spirit, returned from the Jordan and was led by the Spirit in the desert, where for forty days He was tempted by the devil. He ate nothing during those days, and at the end of them He was hungry. The devil said to Him, "If You are the Son of God, tell this stone to become bread." Jesus answered, "It is written: 'Man does not live on bread alone.'" The devil led Him up to a high place and showed Him in an instant all the kingdoms of the world. And he said to Him, "I will give You all their authority and splendor, for it has been given to me, and I can give it to anyone I want to. So if You worship me, it will all be Yours." Jesus answered, "It is written: 'Worship the Lord your God and serve Him only.'" The devil led Him to Jerusalem and had Him stand on the high point

of the temple. "If You are the Son of God," he said, "throw Yourself down from here. For it is written:

'He will command His angels concerning you
   to guard you carefully;
they will lift you up in their hands,
   so that you will not strike your foot against a stone.'"

Jesus answered, "It says, 'Do not put the Lord your God to the test.'" When the devil had finished all this tempting, he left Him until an opportune time. (Luke 4:1–13)

We should learn seven lessons from this account.

1. The enemy often attacks at our weak moments. Jesus was physically weak from His fast.

2. The enemy often attacks the area of our greatest need. Jesus was hungry.

3. The enemy revealed several insights about himself in verse 6. Satan offered to give Jesus, "all their authority and splendor." Jesus is the One who created it all and owns it all. Satan has no authority over Jesus. He is a liar. He is filled with pride. He is blind. But, he often uses truth to attack us! He even quoted scripture.

4. Jesus responded to the devil by quoting scripture in context. That is why we need to hear, read, study, memorize, and meditate on the Word of God. God's Word is our best arsenal to withstand the enemy's attacks.

5. The enemy relies on the same temptations he has used through the ages. He tempted Jesus in the same way he did Adam and Eve: the lust of the flesh (in this case, hunger), the lust of the eye (wealth and splendor), and the pride of life (desire to be in full control, usurping God).

6. Jesus did not respond to the devil's luring. In other words, He did not pick the temptation up and play with it. He did not give it a moment's consideration or imagine what it would be like to give in. Jesus immediately looked to the solution of the situation and dismissed the temptation.

7. We cannot avoid temptation. Even Christ was tempted. But we must look beyond the temptation to our Power Source. As Christians, we are promised, "No temptation has seized you except what is common to man. And God is faithful; He will not let you be tempted beyond what you can bear. But when you are tempted, He will also provide a way out so that you can stand up under it" (1 Cor. 10:13).

SATAN'S PURPOSE REVEALED

Those cute little caricatures that often portray Satan are not realistic. He is the master deceiver, and amusing depictions of him only distort our understanding of him and his intentions. The apostle Peter said, "Be self-controlled and alert. Your enemy the devil prowls around like a roaring lion looking for someone to devour" (1 Peter 5:8). Jesus exposed the devil's purpose: "The thief comes only to steal and kill and destroy" (John 10:10). Nothing about Satan is humorous or cute. His purpose is to keep every person from finding acceptance and forgiveness through faith in the Lord Jesus Christ. He also intends to diminish or destroy the faith of every person who has a personal relationship with God.

Whenever I read that verse in 1 Peter 5, I am reminded of a television show I watched years ago with my family on a vacation. Earlier that morning I had read from 1 Peter 5 for my devotions, and I had paid close attention to Peter's description of

Satan. As we watched *Wild Kingdom* that evening on television, I was especially interested since the program was about lions. It was very informative. The lions we watched did not appear dangerous or threatening. They seemed almost cuddly. I remember commenting, "It would be fun having one of the cubs as a pet." (Needless to say, I have since rethought that idea.)

The lions were tussling and playing in the tall grass. They looked as if they were having a great time. Nearby, a herd of antelope was grazing, totally unaware of the lions. The antelope were also having lots of fun playing together. As I watched the program, I was amazed at the contrast between what I was seeing and the warning I had read in 1 Peter 5 earlier that morning.

The lions and the herd of antelope continued to romp and play. It soon became quite obvious, however, that the lions were not only playing but were also stalking. They quietly circled the antelope herd. Only after the lions eventually isolated one antelope from the herd and positioned themselves for the kill did they roar. But it was too late for the antelope!

Does that situation describe your life? I pray that it doesn't. But if you have been isolated and the enemy is attacking, I pray you will find the principles of this chapter helpful. We do not need to live in fear of Satan, but we must be on our guard and ready for battle. The victory is ours if we put our hope in Christ and rely upon His power to fight the battle.

WHO IS SATAN?

The devil, or Satan, is more than a generic force of evil. He is a living being with supernatural powers that can bring destruction to the world. He is the enemy of the Christian. He has declared war on the Lord Jesus Christ and everyone who claims allegiance to Him.

The name *Satan* is literally translated "deceiver" or "adversary." He is known by many names throughout Scripture: the "tempter" (Matt. 4:3), the "enemy" (Matt. 13:39), the "father of lies" and "murderer" (John 8:44), the "god of this age" (2 Cor. 4:4), among others.

SATAN'S ULTIMATE REBELLION

Satan was an angel, created by God, who became filled with pride and led a rebellion against God's authority. He was thrown out of heaven along with one-third of the angels. When Jesus was commissioning seventy-two disciples to go out on a project of ministry, He alluded to Satan's fall:

> He who listens to you listens to Me; he who rejects you rejects Me; but he who rejects Me rejects Him who sent Me." The seventy-two returned with joy and said, "Lord, even the demons submit to us in Your name." He replied, "I saw Satan fall like lightning from heaven. I have given you authority to trample on snakes and scorpions and to overcome all the power of the enemy; nothing will harm you." (Luke 10:16–19)

Banished from heaven, Satan became the prince of the power of the air who resides in a spiritual realm, along with his demon followers. Far from the funny or ugly representations, he was probably handsome—perfectly created. Yet in his pride and boasting, he stood against the forces of heaven and suffered a horrible punishment.

SATAN'S WAR AGAINST CHRISTIANS

From the moment God banished him from heaven, Satan has been intent on destroying everything dear to God—including God's Son, the Lord Jesus Christ. Satan has tried countless ways to defeat the saving purpose of Christ. He tried to bribe Christ in the wilderness after His baptism and anointing from God. He attempted to turn the world against Jesus' ministry. Satan even had Him betrayed, imprisoned, beaten, and killed. But he failed to eliminate Him. Jesus *won the war!* Jesus forever conquered the devil on the cross: "And having disarmed the powers and authorities, he made a public spectacle of them, triumphing over them by the cross" (Col. 2:15). Jesus rose from the grave, forever victorious over sin's consequence of death and the evil schemes of Satan.

Satan's final outcome is sealed. God has created an eternal and awful residence for the great accuser and his followers: hell. There, he will be bound, suffering its torments forever. Those who have rejected God's offer of mercy and reconciliation through Jesus, choosing to follow Satan, will spend eternity in hell separated from God.

Until then, Satan wages a war against the bodies, minds, and spirits of those who love the Lord Jesus Christ. If you are a Christian ("Christ-one"), you are at war!

God's purpose is to bring humanity into fellowship with Himself. Conversely Satan's purpose is to separate humanity from God. Anything he can do to harden us to His counsel or to entice us away from heavenly things is desirable to Satan. Christians are never exempt from the devil's attacks. While new believers and immature Christians may be susceptible to Satan's temptations to return to old lifestyle habits, experienced and strong Christians may be tempted in different ways.

SATAN'S METHOD OF OPERATION

Satan uses different approaches to achieve his goals. For instance, if a person is firmly committed to Christianity, the devil may not cause forthright doubt in Christ. Instead, he may subtly incite the Christian to sinful anger, lust, bitterness, or another sin that seems hidden. Remember, he is sly. He is conniving. The devil deceives. He plays with our minds, pulls on our heartstrings, and attacks us in our weakest areas.

He delights in putting those in bondage whom Christ has set free. Satan has many tools, such as fear, compulsive habits, self-depreciation, addictions, an unforgiving spirit, and oppression. According to James 1:17, "every good and perfect gift is from above, coming down from the Father of the heavenly lights." Conversely, every bad and imperfect event in our lives is not from God, but from our enemy, Satan.

As human beings, we have the ability to choose: listen to God and obey Him, or give in to Satan's temptations. God calls us with no strings attached. He desires that we obey Him willfully. Satan, however, is the schemer who doesn't care how he manipulates us. He will use any sort of oppression to separate us from God and put us into bondage to himself.

SATAN'S POSSESSION AND OPPRESSION

Satan and his army are truly at work in the world. They seek to oppress and possess the human heart. The Bible gives us many examples of people who were oppressed by Satan's representatives (demons). Although demon possession is less obvious in our culture, there have been verified incidents of its manifestation. There are clear examples of demon possession in the Bible, and those incidents show us a bit more about the character of Satan. Let's notice several of them.

The event recorded in Mark 5 recounts Jesus' healing of a demon-possessed man. When Jesus arrived in the region of the Gerasenes to teach, the man came out to meet Him. Mark told us that "this man lived in the tombs, and no one could bind him any more, not even with a chain. For he had often been chained hand and foot, but he tore the chains apart and broke the irons on his feet. No one was strong enough to subdue him" (Mark 5:3–4).

The man was a miserable, deranged, terrifying creature whom Satan and his demons had mentally, physically, emotionally, and spiritually entangled. Mark continued, "Night and day among the tombs and in the hills [the man] would cry out and cut himself with stones" (Mark 5:5). The demon-possessed man was a threat to the welfare of that society, and he was a threat to his own well-being. The nature of Satan is to destroy humanity.

Another incident of demon possession is seen in Mark 9. A man brought his son to Jesus for healing. The son was "possessed by a spirit that has robbed him of speech. Whenever it seizes him, it throws him to the ground. He foams at the mouth, gnashes his teeth and becomes rigid" (Mark 9:17–18). To imagine this pathetic child's plight stirs deep emotion in us. Jesus was also moved, and He agreed to heal the boy. His healing power is evidence of His power over demons: "When Jesus saw that a crowd was running to the scene, He rebuked the evil spirit. 'You deaf and mute spirit,' He said, 'I command you, come out of him and never enter him again.' The spirit shrieked, convulsed him violently and came out. The boy looked so much like a corpse that many said, 'He's dead.' But Jesus took him by the hand and lifted him to his feet, and he stood up" (Mark 9:25–27).

The threat of danger is real. Demon oppression is a spiritual fact of life: "For our struggle is not against flesh and blood, but against the rulers, against the authorities, against the powers of this dark world and against the spiritual forces of evil in the heavenly realms" (Eph. 6:12).

CHRIST HAS EQUIPPED YOU TO WIN

No matter how solid you are in your beliefs or in your godly lifestyle, you are still susceptible to temptation: "And we have seen and testify that the Father has sent the Son as Savior of the world" (1 John 4:14 NKJV).

The devil is bent on destroying or perverting God's excellent creation. But Jesus has come to reverse the destruction—to put an end to the bondage of sin. Christ's desire is that you have abundant life with Him. But how can you experience abundant life and successfully war against the enemy of your faith at the same time?

1. Learn to Resist the Devil

The apostle James wrote, "Submit yourselves, then, to God. Resist the devil, and he will flee from you" (James 4:7). Jesus Himself modeled this philosophy in His confrontation with Satan in the wilderness (Matt. 4). The enemy tried to trick Jesus into worshiping him. Jesus replied, "Away from me, Satan!" (Matt. 4:10). Notice first that Jesus boldly declared that He would not follow Satan's advice. Resisting the devil means personally resolving not to obey him—declaring your decision that you will not submit to his destructive ways. You will learn that there are common areas where the enemy attacks, based on human weaknesses. You will learn to be alert for Satan's pressure in those areas. Once you encounter his attack, you will learn to stand against it.

2. Depend on the Authority of God's Word

Jesus confronted the devil with this reminder: "It is written: 'Worship the Lord your God, and serve Him only'" (Matt. 4:10). The Son of God used the Word of God as a defensive weapon against Satan's attack. The Bible is your spiritual constitution, declaring your rights as a child of God and God's ownership of your heart. As we have already seen, "To all who received Him, to those who believed in His name, He gave the *right* to become children of God" (John 1:12, emphasis mine).

3. Be Proactive in Your Faith

Peter urged, "Resist him [the devil], standing firm in the faith" (1 Peter 5:9). "Standing firm in the faith" is being about the business of trusting and obeying Christ. Jesus said, "If anyone loves Me, he will obey My teaching. My Father will love him, and We will come to him and make Our home with him" (John 14:23). A soldier at war is vulnerable to the enemy if he is retreating. Victory belongs to those who are pressing forward!

4. Learn to Wield Christ's Spiritual Weapons

The Christian's weapons to counter the devil include regular times of prayer, daily Bible reading, fellowship with other committed Christians, obedience to the principles of the Bible, confession of sin, and constant dependence upon the power of the Holy Spirit. Developing a spiritual regimen that includes private and corporate worship is also an effective way to ward off the enemy's attacks.

5. Put on Christ's Spiritual Armor

Ephesians 6 explains that we have spiritual armor that we can put on to withstand the spiritual attacks of Satan:

> Finally, be strong in the Lord and in His mighty power. Put on the full armor of God so that you can take your stand against the devil's schemes. For our struggle is not against flesh and blood, but against the rulers, against the authorities, against the powers of this dark world and against the spiritual forces of evil in the heavenly realms. Therefore put on the full armor of God, so that when the day of evil comes, you may be able to stand your ground, and after you have done everything, to stand. Stand firm then, with the belt of truth buckled around your waist, with the breastplate of righteousness in place, and with your feet fitted with the readiness that comes from the gospel of peace. In addition to all this, take up the shield of faith, with which you can extinguish all the flaming arrows of the evil one. Take the helmet of salvation and the sword of the Spirit, which is the Word of God. And pray in the Spirit on all occasions with all kinds of prayers and requests. With this in mind, be alert and always keep on praying for all the saints. (Eph. 6:10–18)

Let's look a bit more closely at the spiritual weapons with which God has equipped you. The full armor of God that the apostle Paul wrote about is figurative. The Christian's real enemy is not an earthly, oppressive power or any other physical enemy. The real enemy attempts his destructive rule from a spiritual realm— the "spiritual forces of evil in the heavenly realms" (Eph. 6:12). Subsequently, your armor will not be physical; it, too, will be spiritual.

The first item of protection is the "belt of truth buckled around your waist" (v. 14). It is crucial to be both informed of the truth and loyal to the truth. You cannot stand firm against Satan's deceitfulness if you do not know what is true and what is not. The Bible, God's Word, is your ultimate source of truth. As we have learned, it is a message from God, who cannot lie. As you read, study, and memorize the Bible, you are wrapping yourself in eternal and tested truth.

The "breastplate of righteousness" is the second item (v. 14). Spiritual rightness—godly character—is a strong defense against the enemy. Jesus is prophetically described in Isaiah 59:17 as wearing a breastplate of righteousness. Living righteously guards your heart. Proverbs 13:6 tells us that "righteousness guards the man of integrity, but wickedness overthrows the sinner."

Your feet are to be "fitted with the readiness that comes from the gospel of peace" (v. 15). You need to be ready. Ready to publicly declare your faith. Ready to share the good news with others so they, too, can experience the joy of knowing Christ. Ready to trust in the promises given to you through faith in the Lord Jesus Christ. Peter declared, "Always be prepared to give an answer to everyone who asks you to give the reason for the hope that you have" (1 Peter 3:15). One strong spiritual defense includes being on the alert to declare your trust in Christ.

The "shield of faith" (v. 16) is a weapon that you can use to "extinguish all the flaming arrows of the evil one." From the beginning, Satan's favorite weapon has been doubt (Gen. 3:1). If he can cause you to doubt the instructions or promises of God, he wins a major skirmish. In Roman times, enemies frequently shot flaming arrows. Leather shields could be soaked in water and used to extinguish the fire. The apostle Paul was using this as a figure of speech to tell you that strong faith is a powerful defense.

Faith can put out the fires of doubt. Faith keeps you from wavering in times of testing.

The "helmet of salvation" (v. 17) is the security you have in salvation. If you have accepted Christ as your only means of salvation, then you have already put on a major piece of armor. Through salvation, you now belong to God. God has put His stamp on you, and you are securely His through obedient faith.

The "sword of the Spirit, which is the Word of God" (v. 17) is a strong weapon against the devil. The Word of God contains hundreds of His promises to us. Satan loves to cause us to forget God's revelation of Himself in His Word. Depend on Scripture for spiritual strength and stability. It's a sure way to avoid discouragement. Read God's Word for encouragement. Read it for direction. Read it recreationally; read it devotedly. As you would carry a weapon at all times on the battlefield, always have the Bible at your side.

The apostle Paul wrapped up his list of spiritual armor by exhorting you to "pray in the Spirit on all occasions" (v. 18). Prayer is your direct mode of communication with God. It completes your spiritual uniform. It is true that Satan is real and that he is strong. But God is also real, and He is much stronger than Satan! You do not need to be disabled by fear. Instead, you have confidence that God is already victorious. Access to His power is only a prayer away. The psalmist expressed his confidence in God's accessibility, "I call to the LORD, who is worthy of praise, and I am saved from my enemies" (Ps. 18:3).

Recalling each piece of armor, take a moment to use your imagination. You are sunbathing on the beach when a medieval knight runs up with a quiver filled with arrows. His arrows are not only sharp; they're on fire. He is an expert marksman and takes dead aim at your arm with one arrow and shoots another at your right leg. He then shoots one directly at your heart, and finally he shoots you between the eyes. This is definitely *not* a pleasant picture! It doesn't take much imagination to realize you would soon be dead.

Now, imagine that you are standing on a castle wall, fully clothed in a suit of armor. What happens when this same knight fires his sharp and flaming arrows at you now? They bounce off. You are the same person you were before, but this time you are protected. The armor described in Ephesians 6 is as real as the threats of Satan. Make sure you have it on!

GOD'S PEACE IN THE MIDST OF WAR

Perhaps you are saying, "I don't want to be involved in spiritual warfare! I just want to enjoy the peace of my relationship with God!" The good news is that even in your state of war with the enemy, you can enjoy God's victory and spiritual peace. Since you have the Holy Spirit dwelling inside you, you never need to be without internal peace and confidence in God.

The war is going to continue for a while. In fact, the world will be in a state of constant spiritual turmoil until the day that Christ returns to the earth. After that point in time, those who know Him "will be caught up together . . . in the clouds to meet the Lord in the air. And so we will be with the Lord forever" (1 Thess. 4:17). But Christ has already "disarmed the powers and authorities [of the world, and] made a public spectacle of them, triumphing over them by the cross" (Col. 2:15). You are on the Victor's side. Knowing that, you can proceed in the war with confidence and peace.

YOU AND WORLD EVANGELISM

After His resurrection from the grave, the triumphant Savior, Jesus Christ, spent forty wonderful days with His disciples. The joy that Peter, James, John, and the other disciples felt in seeing their Leader must have been overwhelming. Jesus and His disciples surely reminisced about their ministry together. They probably laughed and wept as they recalled the victories won and the sad rejections that accompanied their travels and outreach.

But the time finally came when Jesus was to leave the earth and return to heaven in preparation for His second coming. He gathered His disciples on a mountaintop overlooking Jerusalem, the Mount of Olives. There He spoke intently to them about their future. He told them He would have to leave them again, and He outlined the work they were to do: "You will receive power when the Holy Spirit comes on you; and you will be My witnesses in Jerusalem, and in all Judea and Samaria, and to the ends of the earth" (Acts 1:8). With that, Jesus ascended to heaven "before their very eyes, and a cloud hid Him from their sight" (Acts 1:9).

This is a restatement of what is known as the Great Commission. There is a passage on the Great Commission in each gospel. I encourage you to read Matthew 28:19–20; Mark 16:15; Luke 24:47; and John 20:21.

The Great Commission is Jesus' parting message to His closest friends and students. It's an exciting exhortation to spread the good news of God's provisions through Jesus' death and the victory of His resurrection.

The disciples had been with Jesus for the past three years. Much had happened. Some, if not all, of them had expected Jesus to overthrow the Romans and set up His kingdom immediately in Jerusalem. They had not understood that He came to die. In the days following His death and resurrection, they had been on an emotional roller-coaster. As they stood on the Mount of Olives that final day, I am sure they felt confusion and fear mixed with their joy and excitement. Although they didn't fully understand where Jesus had been or where He was going, the disciples knew what He wanted them to do.

This command to spread the Good News did not end with the earthly ministry of the disciples. Did you realize your purpose in life is to declare His glory to this generation? We do that through how we live and what we say. Christ redeemed you to be His witness. It is just as important for you and me to declare His message to our society as it was for those first disciples!

New Christians often feel such a great sense of forgiveness and acceptance that they want to share it with the whole world. They know that God has changed their hearts, and they know that they are new persons through faith in the Lord Jesus Christ, but the thought of effectively communicating that experience to their unbelieving families, friends, work associates, or classmates can be intimidating. Where do you start? And how do you share that message of God's love and forgiveness?

THE CALLING

Did you know that as a follower of Jesus Christ, you are automatically called to be a witness? Not every Christian has the specific calling of an evangelist. But if you know Christ in a personal way, He has called you to tell others about the salvation and peace you've found in Him. You may not have a travel itinerary or a crusade director to set up your speaking engagements, but you do have a calling. Jesus said, "I chose you and appointed you to go and bear fruit—fruit that will last. Then the Father will give you whatever you ask in My name" (John 15:16). You are called to be a faithful—and productive—witness.

That spiritual fruit-bearing (productivity) does not show itself only in your manner of conduct and speech. It is also seen in your faithful retelling of the message of the gospel. Maybe you have negative associations with the word *evangelist*. But *evangel* means "the good news." What is that message of good news? You have already discovered it: Jesus died for our sins, was buried and rose again from the dead to give us the hope of everlasting life (1 Cor. 15:1–4).

A witness is someone who tells others what he knows. If Jesus commanded us to be witnesses, we want to make sure we understand what He wants us to do! Let's explore the *what, why, how,* and *where* of being a witness.

WHAT IS EVANGELISM?

Evangelism is doing the work of an evangelist. It is the process of announcing (telling) the good news that Jesus has made a way for everyone who trusts Him to be forgiven of sin and to be assured of an eternal home in heaven. That's not just good news—*it's great news!*

Jesus also used the word *witnessing.* Remember, Jesus said that His followers would be His witnesses. You know from watching TV courtroom dramas that a witness is called to testify about something that he has personally observed. The courtroom witness vows before the court to testify to the truth of his statements. In the same way, a person who has personally witnessed (experienced) God's forgiveness through faith in Jesus Christ is duty-bound to testify about it, especially to those who have not experienced it. Witnessing is testifying about the good news.

Every person who is living in relationship with Jesus Christ is called, commissioned, and ordained by almighty God to be His witness. If this is true—and I believe with all my heart it is—you must be an effective witness. So what is an effective witness? My favorite definition is one Dr. Bill Bright gave years ago: "An effective witness is anybody who takes the initiative to present the claims of Jesus Christ in the power of the Holy Spirit and leaves the results to God." I like this definition because it lets me off the hook. My responsibility—and yours—is to present the message in the power of the Holy Spirit. God will take over from there. He is the One who convicts, calls, and saves.

THE *WHY* OF EVANGELISM

"Why should I be evangelizing?" you may ask. Some people are nervous about sharing what seems to be such a personal issue. Others have been taught, directly or indirectly, not to talk openly about their spiritual experiences. Citing the debate over the separation of church and state, many believe that the sacred and the secular cannot be mixed. But there are several reasons for you to practice verbalizing your faith in Christ.

Jesus Asks You To

As you saw in Acts 1:8, Jesus sent out His disciples with a command: "You will be My witnesses." That doesn't sound like an option, does it? As a follower of Christ, you have pledged in your heart to obey Him—to make Him the Lord of your life. His command is your call to action. Jesus said, "Whoever has My commands and obeys them, he is the one who loves Me" (John 14:21). Obedience is living proof that you have trusted Christ for your forgiveness and acceptance by God.

You Have Something Good to Testify About

You have good news to share! Don't keep it a secret. Jesus said that people do not "light a lamp and put it under a bowl. Instead they put it on its stand, and it gives light to everyone in the house. In the same way, let your light shine before men" (Matt. 5:15–16). In a world that capitalizes on bad news, you have the opportunity to provide a sacred balance. Hoarding the good news is an act of injustice.

Others Desperately Need to Know the Good News

If you have put your trust in Christ as your personal Savior and Lord, you are forgiven and accepted into His family. You personally know what a difference He has made in your life. You acknowledged your need, and Christ met that need with His total forgiveness and adopted you into His family. Your acquaintances may have that same need. Some of those dearest to you—even those living exemplary lives—may be in the same spiritual bondage from which Christ delivered you.

Someone who lives on your street or even in your home needs to know Christ in a personal way. Just like the disciple during Jesus' earthly ministry who brought his brother to Christ, you can introduce others to Him. "Andrew, Simon Peter's brother, was one of the two who heard what John had said and who had followed Jesus. The first thing Andrew did was to find his brother Simon and tell him, 'We have found the Messiah' (that is, the Christ)" (John 1:40–41).

THE *HOW* OF EVANGELISM

As you prepare to witness to others, remember that ultimately you cannot save people. Jesus is the only One who can provide salvation. Your role is to be the instrument through whom Jesus works. You are to carry the message of salvation and demonstrate the proof of salvation, but you cannot convict sinful hearts to change.

The apostle Paul addressed this issue in 1 Corinthians 2:4–5: "My message and my preaching were not with wise and persuasive words, but with a demonstration of the Spirit's power, so that your faith might not rest on men's wisdom, but on God's power." Paul knew that the authority with which he spoke did not come from his wonderful education or speech training. His words greatly influenced people because the Holy Spirit was working through him and speaking to people's hearts. Non-Christians need to place trust in God, not in persuasive speakers.

It is encouraging, however, to realize that God is eager to work through you. According to 2 Chronicles 16:9, "The eyes of the LORD range throughout the earth to strengthen those whose hearts are fully committed to Him." God is looking for people He can use. The prophet Isaiah experienced God working through him. He wrote,

> The Spirit of the Sovereign LORD is on me,
>> because the LORD has anointed me
>> to preach good news to the poor. (Isa. 61:1)

The Holy Spirit is at work in you, and He wants to give you the opportunity to be His instrument in touching the lives of people who need Christ.

Be Prepared Spiritually

When the Holy Spirit prompts you to speak or act, be ready inwardly. How? First, pray. Pray that God will strengthen your willingness to share your faith in Christ. The apostle Paul prayed that the disciples of Christ would be "rooted and built up in Him and established in the faith" (Col. 2:7 NKJV).

Pray that you will have sensitivity to the spiritual needs of others. Some spiritual needs are obvious and others are not. Ask God to impress the needs of others on your heart. Pray that God will move in your friend's heart and that he will recognize his need for God's forgiveness and acceptance. Pray that God will soften your friend's heart to spiritual things and that your friend will hunger for the truth.

Be Prepared Practically

You are to "be prepared in season and out of season" (2 Tim. 4:2). Review how you became a Christian. Think about the positive way the gospel was explained to you, and seek to imitate that style. Listen to other people's experiences in witnessing, and spiritually prepare yourself to be available when the Lord gives you an opportunity to tell someone about the good news.

Some who have been Christians for a long time do not feel adequately prepared to share Christ. Despite their feelings, they obediently respond to the Holy Spirit's prompting and leave the results to Him. All you need is willingness. Your pastor or some other Christian mentor may show you a plan for sharing your faith in Christ, but some of the best witnessing is done from the inside out. God can work miracles through the sincerity of a new believer's testimony, the gentleness that characterizes a believer's actions, and the glow on the face of a person committed to God.

There are times when you'll need a more direct approach. In those cases, the Holy Spirit inside you will do the calling. When you are impressed to verbally explain the gospel to your friend or loved one, you may rely on a variety of evangelism styles; there is no single right format to follow. However, you should include several elements whenever you share your faith with anyone:

1. God loves you.

2. You are separated from God because you cannot live up to His perfect standards. God calls that separation *sin*.

3. There is no human way in which you can be forgiven of that separation.

4. Christ has provided a way of forgiveness through His sacrificial death.

5. You must personally accept Christ as your only way of forgiveness by accepting Him into your life.

Be Prepared Thoughtfully

It is your duty to bring people to Christ, not drive them away. Ask God to help you witness with much tact. Witnessing is both verbal and nonverbal. And witnessing is often a process rather than an immediate action. Some non-Christians will hear the Good News, and others will see the Good News as it is fleshed out in the lives of Christians. Some will gradually come to Christ through a process of hearing, seeing, and acknowledging their needs. For others, it will be a moment of sudden realization. In either case, you are called to take action–to be involved in directly communicating the Good News to non-Christians.

There are some excellent study materials available for you to choose from. But sharing your faith is a bit like learning to ride a bike. You can read all about it. You can watch other people ride bikes, but at some point, you need to get on the bike. How do you begin?

1. Pray! Ask God to give you a burden for those who do not know Christ.

2. Pray! Ask God to direct you to a personal mentor who is an effective witness.

3. Pray! Begin praying for your family, friends, neighbors, and work or school associates who do not know Christ.

If your church offers a training course in effective witnessing, get involved. If your church does not offer a class, talk to your pastor or Sunday school teacher about studying the subject.

One way to learn to become an effective witness is to become involved in a citywide evangelistic outreach. In these joint ventures, many churches come together for the purpose of evangelism and usually offer counselor training. You learn how to share your faith with someone in a loving manner. During the week of evening services, you are given the opportunity to pray with someone who has responded to the call of God. For many people, this is their first experience of actually praying with another individual to receive Christ as Savior and Lord. After having this experience, many people continue to share their faith as a way of life. This is an excellent opportunity to learn how to put the training into action and lead someone to Christ.

THE *WHERE* OF EVANGELISM

In the second part of Acts 1:8, Jesus told the disciples to be witnesses in "Jerusalem, and in all Judea and Samaria, and to the ends of the earth." Let's look at the significance and implications behind these regions.

Jerusalem was the city in which the disciples lived—their home turf. To you and me, Jerusalem may represent our city, home, or place of employment. One important caution: share your faith at your workplace very carefully. Many employers have policies about sharing religious beliefs in the workplace. Many times, your silent witness is just as effective—the way you do your job, interact with others, or pause to thank God for your food.

Your silent witness may prompt someone to seek you out for further questions about your faith. Your response should not be on company time. Make an appointment for a later time, and then share your testimony of God's power in your life.

Judea and Samaria were the regions around Jerusalem. They were general areas of land. They represented the next step. Seek God's wisdom in developing a witnessing plan that extends beyond your comfort zone. That plan may involve being a part of a community witnessing team or a mission trip to another state.

The "ends of the earth" refers to the whole world. Jesus has not only called you to witness in your neighborhood or state; He also wants you to take the Good News wherever He gives you the opportunity, including the whole earth. You may have the opportunity to go on a short-term missions trip, or God may call you to serve as a full-time, vocational missionary.

As you faithfully follow His leading, the Holy Spirit will

guide you in sharing your faith and developing your master plan. We are called to evangelize our world—whether it is our neighborhood or a neighborhood across the globe. If you have received the wonderful, lifesaving Good News, it is now your turn to pass it along.

Words of Encouragement

A primary reason that people do not talk to others about their faith is fear. Who is the author of fear? Satan! God will give you courage, strength, sensitivity, and power if you ask Him. When you pray according to His will, He has promised to hear and answer your prayers. When you pray about witnessing, you can pray with the confidence that you are praying in the perfect will of God.

I do not believe that talking to someone about matters of faith is ever easy. After all, we are discussing the most important decision anyone can make. This is a matter of eternal significance. The conversation will always cause some anxious moments. I still get nervous whenever I share my faith with someone, and I have been sharing my faith one-on-one for more than twenty-five years. It's okay if your Right Guard fails you! I pray that I never am unaffected. This issue is too serious not to show some concern. We are talking about a person's eternal destiny!

You may be interested to know that I have stood in front of a mirror and practiced talking with someone about Christ. Do whatever it takes to get prepared. I suggest you get the booklet *Steps to Peace with God* at your local Christian bookstore. You should practice reading through it until you become comfortable with the entire presentation of the gospel. Then find a Christian friend and take turns making the presentation to each other. Practice! Practice! Practice!

As I said, I have been sharing my faith with others for more than twenty-five years. In all that time, no one has ever gotten mad at me for talking to him about Christ. A few people have declined the offer to talk, and I have honored their request. We need to honor such a request because we are in this for the long haul. People are at different stages of readiness. If I make someone angry, I only make it more difficult for the next Christian God sends to witness to that person. An old saying advises, "You will catch a lot more flies with honey than with vinegar." The same is true of being an effective witness.

The only ability you need to be an effective witness is availability. If you will make yourself available, the Lord will use you in a mighty way. He does not need anything you claim to have. He may choose to use you in a special way because of certain gifts you have, but the key to your usefulness is not your gifts—it's your availability.

When I was in seminary at Trinity Evangelical Divinity School in Deerfield, Illinois, Dr. Arthur Johnston shared the following statement. It has become a favorite of mine, and I hope you will also benefit from it: "If you sow and do not reap, someone will reap after you. Be faithful and keep on sowing. If you reap having not sown, thank God for those that sowed before you and be humble."

God Provides Divine Appointments

We learn from Romans that "we know all things work together for good to those who love God, to those who are called according to His purpose" (8:28 NKJV). If you pray and make yourself available, the Lord will provide you with divine appointments.

It has been a great joy to experience many divine appointments in my lifetime, but I want to share two of my most memorable ones with you. I pray that these stories will encourage you to make yourself available and to pray for divine appointments.

Fifteen years ago when I was in seminary, my family lived in a small suburb of Chicago. My daughter, Michelle, was seven years old, and David, my son, had just had his fifth birthday. Barbara and I had decided we could not afford to go back to Virginia and Pennsylvania for Christmas. We decided we would enjoy Christmas at our home in Highwood, Illinois. It was a difficult decision because it would be the first Christmas we would not spend with our extended families.

You can imagine our excitement when Barb's mom and dad called from Pennsylvania to say they were planning to come to see us after Christmas. It was a wonderful Christmas present!

Michelle and David began to make plans about what they wanted to do when Grandpa and Grandma Beam arrived. They especially wanted to take the train into downtown Chicago to visit several of their favorite places.

It was a cold, snowy January day when we boarded the train and headed for downtown Chicago. Since we rode the train into town, we relied on taxis to travel within the city. Our first destination was the Shedd Aquarium. I hailed a taxi; Barb, Michelle, David, Grandpa, and Grandma piled in the backseat, and I rode in the front seat with the driver.

I have a series of questions I use to start conversations. David had heard me do this many times. My goal is to get to know the individual, and I pray for an opportunity to present the gospel. After I told the driver our destination, I asked him, "Are you originally from Chicago?"

He answered, "I've lived here all my life."

David leaned over the front seat and said, "Ask him, Dad!" I nodded to David, indicating that I planned to.

My next question was, "How long have you been driving a taxi?"

David again said, "Ask him, Dad!"

Evidently I was not getting to the main point quickly enough for David. I tried to continue the conversation and said, "I'm sure you have met a lot of interesting people."

David then leaned over the seat and insisted, "Dad, ask him if he is a Christian!"

"Praise the Lord, brother!" the driver said. "Young man, I thank you for being concerned about my soul! I talk to people about Jesus all the time, but you are the first person to get in my cab and talk to me about Jesus. You keep telling people about Jesus."

Our taxi driver was an inner-city pastor who drove a taxi part-time to earn money and to be a witness. This meeting proved to be a great encouragement for us all.

After our visit to the aquarium, we headed to the Field Museum. When we got in the taxi, we hardly got the doors shut before David said, "Dad, ask him if he is a Christian." Immediately the driver said, "Me Christian!" I could hardly believe my ears. Two taxi drivers in Chicago, and both were believers. Our driver was in Chicago attending graduate school. He was from Korea and was a member of the world's largest church in Seoul. He also encouraged David to continue talking to people about the Lord.

Our next destination was the Sears Tower. When we got in the next taxi, the driver appeared to be in his sixties, and he had the appearance of an alcoholic. Once again, David said, "Dad, ask him if he is a Christian."

The driver had a hard look on his face. Looking straight ahead, he said, "I am an agnostic!"

David said, "What's that, Dad?"

"He believes there is a God, but he doesn't think God can help him," I explained.

"Jesus could save him," David said.

"Yes, David. Jesus could save him," I agreed.

Conversation stopped, and we rode the remainder of the way to the Sears Tower in silence. Everyone got out of the taxi, except me, and when I tried to pay the driver, he said, "I don't want your money." I insisted, but again he refused and said, "You are Christians, and I want to do this to help you." As he talked, tears began rolling down his cheeks. He said, "I ran away from home as a young boy. My mom used to take me to Sunday school and church. Buddy, I am sixty-five years old, and your little boy is the first person in all these years to talk to me about Jesus. I know I need God! Will you pray for me?"

It was my joy and privilege to pray with the taxi driver that cold January day because of the witness of my son. God used a five-year-old boy to lead a sixty-five-year-old taxi driver to Christ. That divine appointment serves as a most memorable day in Chicago for our family.

Another divine appointment took place several years ago. I was on my way to Romania. The Romanian churches had invited me to preach in a number of evangelistic outreaches throughout the country. I boarded the plane and took my seat. Sitting to my left in the window seat was a woman who appeared to be very nervous. I introduced myself, and we began a conversation. After a few minutes she asked, "What do you do?" I told her I was a minister of the gospel. Immediately she said, "Will you pray for me? I am a Christian, but I hate to fly."

I agreed to pray for her. While I was praying, someone sat down to my right. When I finished praying, I saw that it was a young soldier. I said hello to him, and he responded, "Are you a Christian?"

I told him I was, and he said, "Oh, no, I can't believe this." He looked as if he was going to faint, so I promised not to bother him.

He immediately said, "What do you do?"

"I am a minister," I said.

"I can't believe this!" he said. "Do you pastor a church?"

"No, I am an evangelist." I answered.

He exclaimed, "Oh, my God." Then he began to cry.

I asked him to tell me what was wrong. As he tried to talk through his tears, I could hardly believe my ears. He told me that he had been up until after 2:00 A.M. with his dad. His dad was trying to get him to commit his life to Christ before he left for his assignment in Germany. Just after two in the morning, he got mad at his dad and told him, "Leave me alone. I'm going to bed." His dad said, "Mike, you can go to bed, but I am going to ask God to put somebody beside you on that plane who will tell you about Jesus all the way to Germany."

I said, "Mike, are you ready to pray?"

"Yes, sir," he replied.

We prayed even before the plane took off, and I had almost seven hours to do follow-up and get Mike established in his commitment to Jesus. I also went with him to the phone after we landed in Germany. Mike called home to Michigan and told his dad about his commitment to Christ. That is a divine appointment!

God wants to use you as His witness. Make yourself available, and He will provide the divine appointments!

14

PASSING ON THE BLESSING

I have always known blessing as a way of life. In countless words and actions, my parents, brothers and sisters, my godly wife, Barbara, and my two children have affirmed my work and desires. I am a better person today because of their investments in my life. Perhaps you have missed experiencing the joy of this principle at work in your life. I pray that God will help you break from the destructive cycle and that He will bring healing to your life. I hope the principles shared in this chapter will become a way of life for you, and God will use you to be part of the solution to this world's needs as you pass on the blessing.

What is your purpose in life—a degree, marriage, a successful career, brilliant children, and the chance to finally retire in luxury? That is a common, even comfortable, mentality to slip into. But there is much more to life. Maybe you are searching for a specific calling or waiting for an audible sign from God. But God has already declared a purpose for you, for each of us. From the beginning, He specifically blessed humanity (Gen. 1:28). Through His Holy Spirit, God has invested Himself in you as His child for the purpose of declaring His glory.

As I have grown to understand more of the needs around me, I increasingly recognize the need for daily blessings. Blessing is a distinctly spiritual concept. Scripture uses it to describe the divine favor or care conferred by God. When we bless someone, we call for a work of God. Blessing is intended to be a standard lifestyle for Christians because God has redeemed us to bless.

BIBLICAL FOUNDATION OF BLESSING

In Genesis 12, God called Abram. He said some very significant things to Abram that the Jewish community misunderstood. The Lord said to Abram,

> Leave your country, your people and your father's household
> and go to the land I will show you.
> I will make you into a great nation
> and I will bless you;
> I will make your name great,
> and you will be a blessing.
> I will bless those who bless you,
> and whoever curses you I will curse;
> and all peoples on earth
> will be blessed through you. (Gen. 12:1–3)

The Israelites never really grasped that promise. Yes, they understood that God had chosen them. They believed that they had been set apart by God. They believed that they were His chosen people, the apple of God's eye. However, they grew proud with the knowledge and the privilege.

By Jesus' lifetime, if a Samaritan (person of mixed parentage) was walking down the road toward Galilee with the sun beating down from the west and his shadow touched a Jew passing on the opposite side of the road, the Jew would go home to bathe.

Prejudice is certainly nothing new! Somehow the Jewish nation had forgotten God's plan to have all nations blessed through it. Rather than bless people, the Israelites had begun to curse people who were not like them. Today God speaks to the church redeemed by Jesus Christ, but His plan has not changed. In the New Testament, Galatians 3:13–14 explains, "Christ redeemed us from the curse of the law by becoming a curse for us, for it is written: 'Cursed is everyone who is hung on a tree.' He redeemed us in order that the blessing given to Abraham might come to the Gentiles through Christ Jesus, so that by faith, we might receive the promise of the Spirit."

WHAT IS THE BLESSING?

If you know Christ in a personal way, you have been redeemed through faith in Christ so that the blessing God gave to Abraham might come to you. God promised Abraham that He would give him a great name. As Christians through the sacrifice of Jesus, we have even greater names. In every corner of the world at any moment, you will find our brothers and sisters in Christ. God also promised Abraham a land; once again, our blessing is greater. The people of the Middle East are continually fighting over their lands. Yet God has promised us a heavenly land. Jesus described the day when "the King will say to those on His right, 'Come, you who are blessed by My Father; take your inheritance, the kingdom prepared for you since the creation of the world'" (Matt. 25:34). Just as God promised to prosper Abraham (Gen. 12:2), He wants to prosper us.

I am not advocating a gospel that says, "Come to Jesus, and you will have health, wealth, and happiness." We must not westernize the Bible. The gospel of Jesus Christ is universal, and if it is really the gospel, it will work in Harrisonburg, Virginia, Washington, D.C., Romania, Haiti, or anyplace. I cannot imagine walking into a refugee camp and saying, "Name it and claim it!"

Instead, I believe in the "spiritual blessing in Christ" with which Paul said Christians have been blessed (Eph. 1:3). When God promises to bless all nations through us, He tells us that He has redeemed us for the purpose of passing on the blessing. The greatest blessing anyone can receive is salvation through Jesus. When Christ ascended from this earth, He left the Holy Spirit for believers because Jesus has chosen to work through us (Acts 1:8).

God desires to bless us because He loves us and wants to bless all nations of the world through the body of Christ. You have been redeemed through faith in Christ for the purpose of passing on the blessing. You need to remember, "You are not your own; you were bought at a price" (1 Cor. 6:19–20). You belong to Him. You have been grafted into the family of Abraham by faith (Rom. 11).

Some time ago, I was in Pennsylvania with two friends who asked me to play golf with them. You may know that golfers usually play in fours, but that day we had a threesome. Several holes after we began, a man playing alone caught up with our group. We invited him to join us, and he accepted. Each of us introduced himself by his first name. His name was Abe.

As we played through the next few holes together, I began asking Abe the series of questions I use to get to know a person. I usually ask about a person's home, occupation, and interests. My purpose is to find a chance to share the gospel. As I talked with Abe, I found that he had retired after owning a clothing store in Lancaster, Pennsylvania. Several assumptions came to mind. I guessed that maybe his name was really Abraham, and it was.

Later I asked whether he attended church. Abe replied, "I go to synagogue twice a year."

I said, "You're Jewish!"

"Yes," he said.

"I am too!" I responded.

"You are?" he said.

"I am! But Wingfield doesn't sound very Jewish, does it?" I admitted. "Actually, I was adopted."

"Really?" he asked.

"Sure," I said.

It was my turn to hit, so I walked to the tee box. As we moved to the next hole, Abe returned to my story. "So you were adopted? That's wonderful," he said.

"It was the most wonderful thing that I ever experienced," I agreed. "In fact, I don't know what would have happened to me if I hadn't been adopted. My life was pretty messed up. But I was just taken in and accepted, and it totally changed my life."

"What was the name of the family?" he asked.

"Actually it was not a family," I explained. "He was single. He never married."

"Really," he said. "That's amazing."

"Yes, it really is. It changed my life, Abe."

As I took my next turn, I sensed that Abe was fascinated by my adoption. "Well, what was the family name?" he asked again as I returned to the cart.

I paused to look at him. "Abe, I want you to know I'm not kidding you. I'm very serious. You know His name. He's quite famous. Jesus adopted me."

"Do all Christians believe this stuff?" he asked.

"Yes. They might not put it quite like that, but, yes, they do. You see, Abe, I was adopted by faith into the family of Abraham."

God has adopted all of us Christians so that we can bless others. You may pass on the blessing much differently from the way that I have, but God wants to use you to bless someone.

As I explained earlier, I was raised with this principle of blessing, although for years I was unaware of it. About ten years ago, I read *The Blessing,* by Gary Smalley and John Trent. I consider it one of the top ten books that have had an impact on my life in the past decade. As a father of two children, I was especially interested in the book's discussion of the importance of passing on the blessing from one generation to the other. God, the Originator of all blessings, began this tradition as He passed the blessing of Abraham down to Isaac (Gen. 26:12) and Jacob (Gen. 32:29). Whether you are passing blessings to your children and grandchildren, a friend, a work associate, or a neighbor, several principles of blessings apply. As I grow more conscious of my calling to bless and develop these principles, I grow more excited about all the opportunities.

CELEBRATION BLESSINGS

Several years after reading *The Blessing,* I returned to Israel. I was at the Wailing Wall on Thursday, the day that bar mitzvahs are held for Jewish boys. During the bar mitzvah ceremony, a group of men surround the young man, lay their hands on him, and bless him with prayer.

One group of men standing among the crowds next to the Wailing Wall especially intrigued me. A dad, a granddad, and a great-granddad encircled the young man, reaching to him and praying over him. Just as God had instructed them to teach the Law to their children in Deuteronomy 6:4–9, the Jewish men were passing on their faith. I could not understand their Hebrew words, but they were praying fervently. I watched, thinking of the significance of that touch to the son as generations of godly parents blessed him publicly. Such affirmation is powerful in any young person's life.

If you have ever attended a bar mitzvah, you remember the celebration time when the ceremonies conclude. Since access to the Wailing Wall is divided, the women of the family stood above, watching the men pray by the Wall. As soon as the men finished, the women threw candies down onto the men and began cheering. Families and friends dance and whoop celebrating the young man's passage and blessing. As I watched, I wondered why the church does not have a similar time. When someone comes to faith or is baptized, we say, "Amen." I believe these are occasions to celebrate and cheer!

A lot of us find it more natural to party at a football or baseball game. After all, sports have captivated our nation. Don't get me wrong. I enjoy sports, and my wife can attest that at a basketball or football game, I'm among the loudest of the fans. But as important as each championship game is, it doesn't hold eternal value. When someone gives his life to Christ, that is eternally significant. And I believe that such an occasion calls for celebration here on earth too. As the church and as families or individuals, we need to bless these landmarks with celebrations and parties.

While I was considering the implications of these Jewish traditions, I spoke with my friend John Schmid, who ministers in prisons during our Encounter weeks. John, who is a full-time prison evangelist, had just returned from a Bill Glass prison weekend in Florida. Bill Glass, the former pro football player, has probably spoken face-to-face with more prisoners than anyone. He has dedicated his life to sharing the gospel with men and women locked away from our society. John told me about his experiences in Florida with Bill. Florida has one of the largest

Jewish communities in the nation, second only to New York. Fifty thousand men are incarcerated in Florida alone. Of those fifty thousand, only seven are Jewish. More than economic levels, synagogue attendance, or education, Jewish men are distinguished by their formal blessing. At thirteen years of age, a Jewish boy is surrounded by family and friends who lay hands on him, bless him, and celebrate over him.

VERBAL BLESSINGS

We have been raised with a saying that is still alive in elementary schools today. I remember it from my own grade school: "Sticks and stones may break my bones, but words will never hurt me." Maybe you've said it. I don't know who penned those words, but they tell a lie. I can take you to the very spot just outside a school cafeteria in Front Royal, Virginia, where a teacher told me, as a high school freshman, "Wingfield, you always find a way to screw it up!" Words can hurt.

I can also take you to a place in Amherst, Virginia, where I sat in the fourth grade classroom, misbehaving as usual. The teacher came up on my blind side. She clamped her hand on the back of my neck, leaned down, and whispered, "Steve, God has gifted you." Wow! I thought I was in trouble, and she was telling me I was gifted of God! She said, "God has given you a voice that carries really well. One of these days, I believe that He is going to use it in a mighty way." Then she pinched me and added, "But in the meantime, you be quiet." That story may sound humorous, but Mrs. Manoplie used even a bad situation to practice the principle of blessing.

Surrounded by a society of sarcasm and slander, even Christians may be quicker to curse than to bless. Too many churches seem to harbor a spirit of criticism and negative thoughts. But God has called us to light candles of hope and faith, to bless people. Jesus said, "Bless those who curse you" (Luke 6:28).

When I was in graduate school near Chicago, I heard that a fire had destroyed the administration building of my college in Harrisonburg, Virginia. I tried to imagine the campus of Eastern Mennonite College without that central building. Several weeks later, I was speaking at a mission conference in Ohio. In a Mennonite church on Sunday morning, I read a bulletin announcement asking volunteers to come to Harrisonburg to demolish the remains of the administration building. The trustees planned to rebuild on the same site, but could not begin until the debris was cleared away. "No experience necessary," the bulletin said. "Just come. There's something you can do."

A few months later, I was speaking at a church in Virginia for a weekend. On Saturday I had some free time, so I borrowed a car and drove to see my former college campus in Harrisonburg. Construction on the new building had already begun. Steel structures were raised, walls were built, and masons were laying brick. A chain-link fence surrounded the whole project with signs posted every few feet, warning: "Authorized Personnel Only." What made the difference? Just months earlier as they were tearing the building down, all were invited to help. No experience was necessary. But when construction began, only authorized personnel were admitted.

Anyone can curse the darkness, tear down, criticize, murmur, and complain, but God has redeemed us to speak words of love. We are not saved to condemn. In a world of destruction, God calls us to bless. Replace your words of hurt with words of blessing. Jesus often blessed the people with His words. We can return again and again to His words recorded in the New Testament.

Jesus blessed the children (Mark 10:16). His last words on earth were words of blessing (Luke 24:50), and He specifically blessed us, the believers to come (John 20:29).

OCCASIONS FOR BLESSINGS

I look for practical opportunities to bless people, especially my family, in ways beyond words. Be creative as you pray about ways to bless those around you. Besides experiencing the presence of God working through you, blessing people is often fun for the blesser. My wife, Barbara, and I planned occasions to formally bless both of our children, Michelle and David. We developed these ideas throughout their lives, but we processed most of them a little more by the time David was a teenager. We especially wanted to celebrate the fact that our children are believers. They received Christ at very young ages and have never wavered from that decision. We chose their Christian baptism as a special event to bless them with friends and family.

During the spring after he turned fifteen, David came to me and said, "Dad, I think I would like to be baptized. I know I gave my life to Christ, but I want to follow the Lord in baptism." I said, "That's great. I've been praying about it, and Mom and I want to make your baptism a real celebration." I asked David to name five to seven people who had been instrumental in his life. We invited the men and their families to David's baptism and Sunday dinner. "Think of a way that you can bless David," I wrote. "I'm not asking for a gift, although something of symbolic meaning is fine. I just want to use this day to bless my son."

We had a wonderful day beginning with the morning baptism at church.. Following the meal in our home, we set a chair in the center of a room for David. I stood with the men around him, and we took turns blessing him. David is the youngest of my parents' grandchildren, and since my mom and dad are in heaven, I blessed him on their behalf. I reminded David how much my dad loved him. I reminded him of how Papa and Mama Wingfield had prayed for him. I told David the phrase my dad told me whenever I left home: "Remember who you are and whose you are."

David's other granddad blessed him with words from Timothy, encouraging him not to be ashamed of his youth. He said that ever since David was born, he believed that God had a plan for his life and that God was going to use him. Our pastor then blessed him with the name David. He had researched the symbolism behind King David, a man after God's own heart. David's best friend's dad gave him a knife, symbolizing that God's Word is sharper than a two-edged sword. David's fifth grade Sunday school teacher blessed him with a word, saying, "When I think of faithfulness, I think of David Wingfield."

My niece's husband, Andrew, and David were good friends. They often played basketball or hung out together. When Barbara and I were out of town, Beth and Andrew stayed at our house with Michelle and David. On the afternoon of David's blessing, Beth and Andrew had recently had their first child. For the first time they told us that they had decided not to have children, but changed their minds after spending time with Michelle and David. Andrew said, "David, I'm a dad because of you. You have blessed me, and now I bless you." We concluded our time of blessing by praying for David. After our prayers, I gave David a relay baton, symbolizing the passing of faith from one generation to the next.

Your method of passing on the blessing may be totally different. The form is not the important part. It is the principle.

Make time to bless those around you. Make passing on the blessing a way of life.

RELATIONAL BLESSINGS

One of the great needs of this generation is relational. I am
thankful to God for two godly men in my life, Howard Smith
and Ray Hurdley. Both of them are in heaven today, but when
I knew them as a young teen, they would probably have
described themselves only as laymen. Howard was a fisherman
on the eastern shore of Virginia and Ray owned a seafood business. As the youngest of seven children with all four brothers in
the ministry, I went through a rebellious time. Looking back, I
understand my teenage years as an identity crisis, but I acted it
out as rebellion against the Lord and I rejected the ministry.
During that time, Howard Smith and Ray Hurdley quietly
blessed me. On many Sunday mornings, following the worship
services at our church, one of them would come up and put his
arm around me as we walked from church. Sometimes he only
said, "Steve, I just want you to know I believe in you." Howard
and Ray were demonstrating their love for me. Somehow today,
the relational aspects of blessing are especially easy to drop.
They take time, but relational investments are an imperative
aspect of blessing.

Relational blessings are the same mentoring principles that
Jesus used with His disciples. Throughout the Gospels, He
demonstrated an inconceivable breadth of patience with those
twelve men, and He simply spent time with them. For three
years, Jesus lived with them through countless daily experiences.
In our lives, God has naturally built in the same opportunities to
impart blessings over the long term.

PRACTICAL KEYS TO BLESSING

Whether it's a party, an encouraging word, a special occasion, or a long-term relationship. Here are some helpful keys to blessing.

Meaningful Touch

Touch is really important. Visiting a retirement community always reminds me of the desire for positive touch. Physical contact is humanizing, even healing. As I talk and counsel with persons who have lost a mate, many of them have told me that one of the most difficult things to deal with is not having someone to touch them. When you offer a hug or put your hand on someone's shoulder, you bless him. You may be saying, "I'm just not the hugging and touching kind." My advice to you is, "Get over it." This is important.

Spoken Words

You can choose to curse or to bless. Isn't it sad that sometimes we curse and discourage those who are dearest to us? We would never say those things before a group of friends or our church. The most difficult place for me to be filled with the Holy Spirit is within the walls of my home with the people who know me best and love me most. God has redeemed us to bless them, not curse them; to build them up, not tear them down.

A Special Future Visualized for That Person

Aren't you thankful that someone saw in you not just who you were, but who you could be? Today you are a better person because someone came beside you and blessed you. Simply by believing in someone, you may see potential that he does not recognize. That's what God has done for you and desires to do through you. You have been redeemed to pass on the blessing.

Active Commitment to the Other Person's Success

You are who you are today because of the people who invested themselves in you—maybe your parents, your grandparents, a teacher, a pastor, an employer, or a friend. They saw potential in you as a person, and they committed themselves to helping you become who you are today.

God says, "All peoples on earth will be blessed through you" (Gen. 12:3). Since Christ gave the Holy Spirit to remain within believers here on earth, we are equipped with the materials for blessing. Paul described the "fruit of the Spirit" (Gal. 5:22–23). The fruit are also the marks of blessing: "love, joy, peace, patience, kindness, goodness, faithfulness, gentleness and self-control." Begin by loving the Lord your God with all your heart and your neighbor as yourself. When this world threatens to rob you of joy, peace, and courage, "do not be conformed to this world, but be transformed by the renewing of your mind" (Rom. 12:2 NKJV). Through these gifts of the Spirit, you can bear the fruit of blessing.

HOW TO GET STARTED

- Make a list of at least four people you personally know.

- Begin praying for them daily.

- Look for ways to bless them (through meaningful touch, spoken words, seeing not just who they are, but who they can be in Christ).

- Share with them what Christ means to you personally.

- Invite them to an evangelistic event where they will have the opportunity to hear the gospel.

Continue to look to the Bible for examples of blessing. Scripture is a portfolio of positive models to learn from as we practice blessing. God pronounced words of blessing over Abram. God set aside Jesus at His baptism to pronounce a special blessing over Him. Jesus began His ministry of blessing at a place of celebration, the wedding at Cana. Even Jesus' daily interaction with and discipleship of the twelve men He handpicked to teach were forms of blessing.

I challenge you to be a blessing. God has placed you in your family, your church, and your world to be an instrument of His blessing. I pray these principles will become a way of life. Your family and friends are the most important things in your life. Cherish these relationships, and heal divisions as they arise. After King David brought the ark of the Lord into Jerusalem, he "returned home to bless his family" (1 Chron. 16:43). Perhaps you need to return to bless your home too. If you have not blessed especially those closest to you, don't go through today without speaking words of blessing. Some of us have a hard time saying "I love you." Yet we all need to hear it. I encourage you to say it, even by phone. I travel a lot, but when I call home one of the last things I tell my son or my daughter is, "I love you and I believe in you." Children need to hear that no matter what anyone else thinks. You believe in them. When my wife, Barbara, and I speak by telephone, I end the conversation with "I love you." As Christians, we are called to bless people far beyond our families, but your family is a great place to begin practicing the principles of blessing.

The three most important relationships in life are faith (your relationship to God), family, and friends. Cherish and protect these relationships at all costs. They are your most valuable possessions. When you pass on the blessing to your family and friends, you bless the Lord.

Remember, the Lord wants to use you to pass on the blessing. Whatever you do today and for the rest of your life, that is your purpose on this earth. Live the adventure by passing on the blessing.

Pray, "Lord, speak into my life. I pray that from this day I will be an instrument of Your blessing in the midst of a world of darkness. Use my life as a light to reflect the light of Your presence for a world that desperately needs to see the glory of Your love. May I be available for You to love others through me. May the world in which I live be blessed because of Your presence in me. In the wonderful, powerful, and matchless name of Jesus I pray. Amen."

15

KNOWING THE WILL OF GOD

Can I really know God's will for my life?" "Do you think God really has a plan for my life?" "How do I know that what I'm doing is God's will?" "Does His will change?" "Does God have something special for me to do?" These are some of the questions I often hear. I believe they're also some of the most important and serious questions a Christian can ask.

Without any reservations, I believe God has a plan for your life. I also believe He wants you to live with peace and assurance that you are in the center of His will. Yes, you can know the will of God!

Living from day to day may feel much like visiting a major city for the first time without a map. Suddenly you realize you don't know where you are or how to get to where you should be. You know there is a way to your destination, but there are so many alternate routes!

Sometimes living from day to day feels like driving through a blinding snowstorm. You feel as if everything is coming at you all at once. There are so many choices! Which way do you go? Far from being focused and at peace, you grow more confused by the moment. Your life is full of uncertainty and anxiety.

College students may change their majors at least three times and stretch a four-year degree into six. In the fast-changing world in which we live, it has become the norm to switch career paths several times. Seminaries across America reflect this trend. The majority of students in some of America's leading seminaries are people who are in midlife career changes.

Where is God in all this change?

Let's revisit the big city. You don't know where you are or where you are going. What do you do? People react to this situation in different ways. Some panic: "Help! I don't know where I am or where I'm going!" Panic, however, will not help you find your way. It only adds to your frustration and insecurity.

You may sit down on a park bench or the step of a high-rise building, waiting for an impulse to hit you—a gut feeling about the right direction. The problem with gut feelings is that they are not always dependable; they are as changeable as the weather. They could be caused by that pizza you had for lunch!

Eventually, you may ask someone for directions. But doing this can be risky. I remember going to a conference in Washington, D.C., years ago with three friends. I was driving, but none of us knew exactly where we were going. We had a general idea, and we knew we were getting close, but the map and directions were in my suitcase in the trunk. Of course, I should have stopped, opened the trunk, and found the map and directions. Our problem would have been solved. But it was late at night, and we were lost in downtown Washington, D.C.

I break the male image of refusing to ask for directions. If I don't know where I am, I ask for help. Why bother with a map when you can ask? I am also a fairly trusting kind of guy. So we stopped at a traffic light and a car pulled up beside us. I rolled down my window, and I asked the man in the car how to get to the conference hotel. He said, "That is where the woman in front of you is going. Just follow her!" I thanked him and began following the car in front of me. About twenty minutes later, the woman in front of me was scared to death, and I realized that I had been completely fooled.

Be careful whom you ask for directions! For me, the situation ended with lots of laughs for everyone in my car. (Even though none of them had questioned the plan to follow the vehicle in front of us.) The guy who gave me the directions is probably still telling the story and getting lots of laughs, just as I do.

If you don't ask for directions, another option is to find a map or written directions. You still may need to ask for help, but you can verify what you are being told. Both are important!

Use your imagination for a moment. You are sitting on a park bench or the step of that high-rise building. Jesus comes and sits down beside you. Once you recover from the shock of realizing that this really is Jesus, He says, "I will answer one question for you." What would you ask Him?

I think most people would ask a question that relates to knowing the will of God for their lives. Especially for those of us who know Christ in a personal way, this is the most important question we can ask: "Lord, what is Your will for my life? What do You want me to do?"

GOD HAS A PLAN FOR YOU

A great joy of being a Christian is knowing that God has a purpose for your life and that you can be part of His plan for now and eternity. One of my favorite Bible verses is this, "For we are God's workmanship, created in Christ Jesus to do good works, which God prepared in advance for us to do" (Eph. 2:10). These are awesome statements! You are carefully crafted by God. Through Jesus' sacrifice, you are created to do good works, works that God has already prepared for you to do. Take some time to meditate on these truths. Let them sink into your mind and soul. You are an important and significant part of God's plan for this world.

David said, "If the LORD delights in a man's way, He makes his steps firm" (Ps. 37:23). In Acts 13:2, we read, "While they were worshiping the Lord and fasting, the Holy Spirit said, 'Set apart for Me Barnabas and Saul for the work to which I have called them.'"

Just as God called men and women throughout the Bible, He has a plan for each of us, and He has promised to reveal it to us. In Psalm 73:24, David said to God, "You guide me with Your counsel, and afterward You will take me into glory." In Psalm 32:8, read God's promise to you as His child: "I will instruct you and teach you in the way you should go; I will counsel you and watch over you." The Lord spoke to the prophet Isaiah,

> This is what the LORD says—
> your Redeemer, the Holy One of Israel:
> "I am the LORD your God,
> > who teaches you what is best for you,
> > who directs you in the way you should go." (Isa. 48:17–18)

Proverbs 3:5–6 is an especially powerful promise:

> Trust in the LORD with all your heart
> > and lean not on your own understanding;
> in all your ways acknowledge Him,
> > and He will make your paths straight.

GOD'S GUIDE AND A ROAD MAP

If you're going to find your way, its helpful to have two things: (1) a guide—someone who is experienced, who knows how to direct you from where you are to where you ought to be; and (2) a map—something that will pinpoint your location and give you alternate routes (based on the wisdom of those who have found their way and have left instructions for future travelers).

As a follower of Jesus Christ, you have both. The Holy Spirit is your Guide. Jesus promised that when He ascended to heaven, He would send us His Spirit to be our constant companion: "When He, the Spirit of truth, comes, He will guide you into all truth" (John 16:13). The Bible is your map. An experienced traveler wrote,

> Your word is a lamp to my feet
>   and a light for my path . . .
> Direct my footsteps according to Your word. (Ps 119:105, 133)

Anyone who is sincere in Christ and truly desires to live by God's standard knows that life is made up of a series of important choices—career choices, relationship choices, financial choices, and many others. God proactively helps you with these choices: "In his heart a man plans his course, but the LORD determines his steps" (Prov. 16:9).

God has a vision for your life. He not only knows where you are; He also knows where you ought to be—the place(s) that will give you a sense of purpose and peace. "For I know the plans I have for you," declares the Lord, "plans to prosper you and not to harm you, plans to give you hope and a future" (Jer. 29:11). God is not some cosmic force or a vague spirit; He is a personal

Friend and Savior. He has a master plan for the universe, and He has a personal plan for your life.

When He walked on the earth, Jesus was in tune with His heavenly Father's will: "For I have come down from heaven, not to do My own will, but the will of Him who sent Me" (John 6:38 NKJV). As Jesus prayed in the Garden of Gethsemane just before His betrayal and death, the Bible says, "He fell with His face to the ground and prayed, 'My Father, if it is possible, may this cup be taken from Me. Yet not as I will, but as You will'" (Matt 26:39). Even in Christ's life, doing the will of God is not always fun and easy, but it is always best.

GOD'S WORD REVEALS GOD'S WILL

Much of God's will has already been revealed through His Word, the Bible. As we have seen earlier, it is God's will that every person become His child through faith in the Lord Jesus Christ. God does not want "anyone to perish, but everyone to come to repentance" (2 Peter 3:9). Scripture also reveals a master plan for carrying out that purpose. Jesus Christ became our substitute and died on the cross for our sins. He "gave Himself for our sins to rescue us from the present evil age, according to the will of our God and Father" (Gal. 1:4).

There are times when God's plan is clearly defined—there is specific direction based on the instruction of His Word, His Spirit's confirmation, and the affirmation of fellow Christians. For example, it is God's will that we should be forgiven of our past and receive the hope of eternal life through faith in Christ, and it has been revealed that we should live our lives on the earth in a pure and holy manner:

Now we ask you and urge you in the Lord Jesus to do this more and more. For you know what instructions we gave you by the authority of the Lord Jesus. It is God's will that you should be sanctified: that you should avoid sexual immorality; that each of you should learn to control his own body in a way that is holy and honorable, not in passionate lust like the heathen, who do not know God; and that in this matter no one should wrong his brother or take advantage of him. The Lord will punish men for all such sins, as we have already told you and warned you. For God did not call us to be impure, but to live a holy life. (1 Thess. 4:1–7)

God's Word reveals His will for our attitude in certain situations: "Give thanks in all circumstances, for this is God's will for you in Christ Jesus" (1 Thess. 5:18). He has even told us how we should face our critics: "For it is God's will that by doing good you should silence the ignorant talk of foolish men" (1 Peter 2:15).

The purpose of the Bible is to reveal God's character, and you can be certain that God's vision for you will never be contrary to His revealed character. Since God is love, it would never be God's will for a Christian to neglect his children. Nor would it be God's will for a Christian to react with sinful anger to frustrating situations. God reiterates His value of human life—made in His own image—throughout the Bible, so it is not God's will to demean or disregard any human life. It is never God's will for you to be rudely impatient because Scripture tells us that God is patient. If your actions (or reactions) are not characteristic of God, you know that they are not within His will.

It is human nature to make decisions based on past experience. God's Word also demonstrates that we can prepare for our future by examining how God has worked in our past and the past experiences of others. As God revealed His plan for His people in the Old Testament, He advised them to face the future, remembering what He did for them in the past. God told their leader, Joshua, to remind them of how He miraculously delivered them:

> Joshua called together the twelve men he had appointed from the Israelites, one from each tribe, and said to them, "Go over before the ark of the LORD your God into the middle of the Jordan [river]. Each of you is to take up a stone on his shoulder, according to the number of the tribes of the Israelites, to serve as a sign among you. In the future, when your children ask you, 'What do these stones mean?' tell them that the flow of the Jordan was cut off before the ark of the covenant of the LORD. When it crossed the Jordan, the waters of the Jordan were cut off. These stones are to be a memorial to the people of Israel forever." (Josh. 4:4–7)

If you want to know God's will for a particular situation, you need to get into the Word of God. Your past experience may not always be an accurate guide, but the Scriptures will always be. God may not address your situation directly, but He always has a word of direction from the Scriptures for you.

A PARTNERSHIP WITH GOD

God's revealed will is a standard that He wants His people to live up to. Only we can truly know God's will. When you accepted Christ as your Savior, you entered into a partnership with God. You have a living relationship with the Creator of the universe. You know God's character and learn to seek His vision in a way that a nonbeliever never could. John told us that "God does not listen to sinners. He listens to the godly man who does His will" (John 9:31). John also explained that the person who is truly devoted to God will welcome Jesus' teaching (John 7:17).

Paul wrote, "Do not conform any longer to the pattern of this world, but be transformed by the renewing of your mind. Then you will be able to test and approve what God's will is— His good, pleasing and perfect will" (Rom. 12:2). Paul made it clear in this passage that we must be transformed by the renewing of our minds. Jesus is the only One who transforms lives. We must be changed by Him to know God's will with certainty. We also need to obey God's known will—the expectations He has made clear through His Word, His Spirit, and His people.

A PROCESS REVEALS GOD'S WILL

Sometimes, discerning God's will is a process with various—perhaps difficult—steps. It would be easier to have direct instructions for identifying God's vision. For example, God gave Noah exact measurements for building the ark. God also gave Moses very precise measurements and instructions to build the tabernacle (the Old Testament place of worship before Jerusalem's temple was built). Each man knew exactly the measurements of his project—right down to the very inch.

Many of us today wish that God would give us precise instructions—how to know which job we should have, how to raise godly children, or how to decide on a marriage partner. But the fact is, God does not always give such detailed instructions. When He told Abram to leave his home country and travel to the promised land, God said, "Leave your country, your people and your father's household and go to the land I will show you" (Gen. 12:1). That is not a very detailed travel plan! Christians need to recognize that God's will is not always a specific set of directions. Sometimes God decides to reveal stages of His plans along the journey, as He did with Abram.

FIVE GUIDELINES FOR
DISCERNING GOD'S WILL

Yet as Christians, we can take several steps to identify God's will. When I was in college through the early 1970s, I asked the president of Eastern Mennonite College, Dr. Myron Augsburger, "How do you know you are doing the will of God?" His unforgettable answer has proved invaluable in my walk with Christ as I have lived the adventure of knowing and following Christ for more than twenty-five years. These five guidelines have become such an integral part of my life that I go through the list with almost every decision I make. I pray that they will be helpful for you too.

1. Obey God's Word

The vast majority of God's will for your life has already been revealed in His Word. God will never ask you to do anything contrary to His Word. You already know there is nothing in the Bible that gives you personal instruction for a specific career choice, but there are numerous commands for other aspects of your personal life. If His Word has spoken, you need not look any farther for the will of God. The matter is settled. Just obey!

2. Ask God What His Will Is for You

Prayer is vitally important in your search for God's will. The Bible consistently teaches us to ask God for His will. The psalmist prayed,

Teach me to do Your will,
 for You are my God;
may Your good Spirit
 lead me on level ground. (Ps. 143:10)

God will not always reveal His will to you immediately, even after you pray about it. However, you can be sure that God will reveal as much of His will to you as you need at the present time. God wants you to have all the information necessary for your life. Sometimes you have to operate on faith when, in your finite understanding, you feel that you should know more than He has revealed. God guides according to His superior plan. In the meantime, feel free to ask God for His will to be accomplished, even if you're not sure exactly what it is! Let Him know you want to be in the center of His will for your life.

One of the marks of a mature believer is praying for God's will to be done and meaning it. Jesus modeled that in His prayer before His death on the cross.

They went to a place called Gethsemane, and Jesus said to His disciples, "Sit here while I pray." He took Peter, James and John along with Him, and He began to be deeply distressed and troubled. "My soul is overwhelmed with sorrow to the point of death," He said to them. "Stay here and keep watch." Going a little farther, He fell to the ground and prayed that if possible the hour might pass from Him. "Abba, Father," He said, "everything is possible for You. Take this cup from Me. Yet not what I will, but what You will." (Mark 14:32–36)

Jesus aligned Himself with His heavenly Father's will. Likewise, God desires that you adjust yourself to Him through prayer.

Remember, Jesus taught us to pray, "Your kingdom come, Your will be done on earth as it is in heaven" (Matt. 6:10).

As you grow in your Christian life, you will come to realize that prayer often changes you. When you pray, "God, Your will be done, not mine," you are showing your commitment to follow Christ and let Him be the Leader. If that is the intent of your heart, ask in prayer for God's will in your life. First John 5:14 is a promise to those who are willing to seek God's will in prayer: "If we ask anything according to [God's] will, He hears us."

We live in a fast-food culture—we want things now rather than later, and the quicker, the better! But our frantic schedules have left us empty and feeling frazzled and unfulfilled. The Bible encourages us to "be still" (Ps. 46:10). God operates on a totally different time-clock from ours. His Word says, "Do not forget this one thing, dear friends: With the Lord a day is like a thousand years, and a thousand years are like a day. The Lord is not slow in keeping His promise, as some understand slowness. He is patient with you" (2 Peter 3:8–9).

God's clock keeps perfect time. At just the right time, if you are paying attention, God will reveal His will to you.

3. Recognize that His Spirit Bears Witness

When you trusted Christ as your Savior, the Holy Spirit began living in you. (See Chapters 9 and 10.) Before His return to heaven, Jesus said, "I will ask the Father, and He will give you another Counselor to be with you forever—the Spirit of truth. The world cannot accept Him, because it neither sees him nor knows him. But you know Him, for He lives with you and will be in you" (John 14:16–17).

The Holy Spirit lives in you to help you with the decisions of life. He "bears witness" (interacts) with your spirit so you can know that you are in the center of God's will. One fruit of the Spirit is peace. God wants His children to experience the peace of God as a way of life. When you are doing God's will, you experience serenity, even when a storm is raging around you.

4. Heed Circumstances

God opens doors (opportunities), and He closes doors. Because you are His child, He has promised to direct your steps. For you, life is not a series of accidents, based on chance or happenstance. You are not some insignificant blob. The Bible says, "We know that in all things God works for the good of those who love Him, who have been called according to his purpose" (Rom. 8:28). You can trust God. He did not say *some* things; He said *all* things. He will direct all your circumstances. This does not mean that you should sit around and wait for things to happen, but it does mean that God speaks and directs your steps through the circumstances of life.

5. Have a Relationship with the Body of Christ

When you trusted Christ as your Savior and Lord, you were brought into a new relationship with Him and others who know and serve Him. You are now part of the body of Christ. That body is made up of "every nation, tribe, language and people" (Rev. 14:6). What a fellowship!

A key element of spiritual growth is your relationship with the body of Christ. I have found that it is very helpful to have an accountability relationship with several people in the body. Your church congregation is part of that accountability relationship, but I encourage you to be involved in an accountability relationship with a small group also. One of the ways God speaks to us is through those who are closest to us in the body, the Christians who know us best. For me, these people include my wife, Barbara, and my children, Michelle and David. I also have several close friends who help me discern God's will in particular situations.

How does it work?

1. You need to read the Bible. (God will never ask you to do anything contrary to His Word.)

2. You need to pray and ask for His direction in the matter.

3. He gives you peace regarding the situation.

4. The circumstance is clear; you have the opportunity to do something.

5. Your close friends in the body of Christ affirm this situation as being God's will.

When all of these guidelines affirm a decision, it is a clear indication of God's will. You can step forward with confidence that you are doing the will of God. If one of these five is not in agreement, you should consider that as a yellow warning light from God. It may not mean that the choice in question is absolutely out of God's will for you; it just may not be the right time.

In 1989, a friend made it possible for me to bring my son on a trip to Romania. David was nine years old, and we both were looking forward to this special time together. It was to be an eighteen-day trip.

I had been in communist Romania the year before, and as a result of that trip, a number of Romanian church leaders had invited me to return. On the past trip, I had the joy, honor, and privilege to see the mighty hand of God working among His people in amazing ways. On this trip, I was to preach in churches throughout Romania. As you have already read, the Romanian church has made a major impact on my life and ministry. I wanted my son to have this same experience. We planned to depart for Romania on December 28, 1989.

You may remember that the revolution began in Romania on December 16, 1989. At first, it looked as though we would be unable to make the trip; the border was closed because of the fighting and upheaval. I tried to stay informed about the situation, and several friends urged me to travel to Europe to be available if the border opened. The Romanian church would be in great need, and my friends felt that the Lord would want me to be there as an encouragement to the body. With this counsel, the team began to make last-minute arrangements and prepared to make the trip.

On the night before we were to fly to Vienna, Austria, David and I were packing our suitcases when the phone rang. It was a close friend from Pennsylvania. He called to let me know he was praying for me, and then he asked, "Are you still planning to take David with you?" My response was an immediate yes. He then said, "As I was praying, I felt the Lord say to me, 'David should not go.'" I thanked my friend for his concern, but assured him that David would be going. Again he said, "I don't think he should go."

When I hung up, I tried to shake off the uneasy feeling I was having because I really wanted David to accompany me on this trip. I had not yet told Barb, Michelle, or David about my phone conversation. As I was going through this inner turmoil, the phone rang again. This time it was a friend from Roanoke, Virginia. He told me he would be praying for my trip, and then he said, "Steve, as I was praying about your trip, I felt the Lord say to me, 'David should not go with Steve on this trip.'" My immediate response was, "Have you been talking to Ike?" I already knew what his reply would be: "No, I haven't talked to anyone."

Was the decision easy? Yes and no!

The easy part was, I believed God had clearly spoken to me through my friends. I had no question that it was God's will that David should not go with me on the trip. Not only had God spoken through my friends, but I no longer had peace about taking David on the trip.

The hard part was conveying a life principle like this to a nine-year-old boy who was looking forward to a big trip with his dad. The other hard part was allowing my emotions to catch up with the will of God for my life. God's will in this matter was not my will. I really wanted David to go! In all honesty, I struggled with the decision for the first week of travel in Romania. It was awesome, and I must admit that I was emotionally frustrated with God, and with my friends Ike and Bill, who I felt had deprived David and me of this wonderful experience together.

Only after arriving in Timisoara (where the revolution began) did I understand why it was not God's will for David to be with me on the trip. It was an extremely difficult time, one of the most demanding of my Christian experience. At one point, I thought we might not get out of Romania alive. It appeared that the fighting might start again. I saw and experienced things that no nine-year-old should ever have to experience. In a frigid hotel room in Timisoara, Romania, I repented of my attitude. I thanked God for working through my friends who helped me conform to the will of God.

GOD'S AGENDA, NOT OURS

We are often too eager to get on with doing God's work, bypassing God's plans and plowing ahead with our agendas. But God has one supreme agenda. He has a perfect plan that you can align your life with. God doesn't automatically detail all the answers for your life situations upon request. He wants you to join His eternal agenda. (Yours is short-range.) Learning God's agenda takes time.

One of the best ways to get started and to learn how to discern God's will is to act on what you know. A good rule of thumb when seeking to know God's will in a particular situation is to obey as much as you can. Be like the Old Testament leader Abram, who had no idea where on earth God wanted him to move, but started packing. Perhaps God wants you to start packing before He tells you what the next move will be. There will always be at least a small step that you can take in the direction of God's will. Demanding to know the start, finish, and everything in between of your journey with God will not get you anywhere. You must just aim for Point A. Once you have reached Point A, then God will direct you toward Point B. You may never actually know your final destination until you reach Point Z—your eternal home in heaven.

What would Jesus do? *WWJD?* That's been a popular question in the last few years. Perhaps a better question is, *What would Jesus have me do?* It is important to ask these questions and earnestly seek the will of God. But your response should always be *DWJD!* Do what Jesus did!

NOTES

CHAPTER 1
1. Erica Noonon, "All 3 Bodies Found at JFK Jr. Crash Site," <HoustonChronicle.com>, 21 July 1999, Breaking News section.

CHAPTER 7
1. Dr. John R. W. Stott, *Understanding the Bible* (Glendale, CA: Gospel Light Publications, 1972).
2. Dr. A. W. Tozer, *The Root of the Righteous* (Harrisburg, PA: Christian Pub., 1955).
3. Stott, *Understanding the Bible.*

CHAPTER 9
1. People for the Ethical Treatment of Animals Web site <http://www.milksucks.com/bearsurvey.html>.

CHAPTER 15
1. Stott, *Understanding the Bible.*

ABOUT THE AUTHOR

STEVE WINGFIELD serves as President of Wingfield Ministries, Inc., an organization dedicated to assisting the church in reaching the world of Jesus Christ.

Steve has conducted major inter-denominational evangelistic crusades across the United States and overseas for 15 years since founding Wingfield Ministries. Through Encounter crusades, thousands have been led to a personal relationship with Jesus Christ. Steve frequently speaks at retreats, universities and special events, and has trained thousands of believers to share their faith. At Tyndale Theological Seminary of Amsterdam, Netherlands, he teaches "Introduction to Evangelism: and is a frequent guest speaker at the Billy Graham Center in Wheaton, Illinois.

He pastored in Roanoke, Virginia, for seven years, hosting a daily radio broadcast and founding the Roanoke Ministerial Association. He is a graduate of Trinity Evangelical Divinity School and Eastern Mennonite College. At Trinity, he served as Teaching Assistant to Dr. Robert Coleman, author of the classic volume *The Master Plan of Evangelism*.

In recognition of his leadership in Christian evangelism, he has been listed in *Outstanding Young Men of America, Outstanding Religious Leaders of America, Who's Who in American Christian*

Leadership, Who';s Who in America, Who's Who in Religion in America, and *Who's Who in Methodism.*

Steve resides with his wife, Barbara, in Mt. Crawford, Virginia. They have two grown children, Michelle and David.